Techniques an
Strategies
for Financing
and Valuing Your
Small Business

HOW TO
RAISE
CAPITAL

Jeffry A. Timmons, Stephen Spinelli, and Andrew Zacharakis

McGraw·Hill

New York   Chicago   San Francisco   Lisbon   London   Madrid   Mexico City
Milan   New Delhi   San Juan   Seoul   Singapore   Sydney   Toronto

Library of Congress Cataloging-in-Publication Data

Timmons, Jeffry A.
   How to raise capital : techniques and strategies for financing and valuing your small business / by Jeffry A. Timmons, Stephen Spinelli, Andrew Zacharakis.
       p.   cm.
   ISBN 0-07-141288-3 (pbk. : alk. paper)
       1. Small business—Finance.   2. New business enterprises—Finance.
   3. Venture capital.   I. Spinelli, Stephen.   II. Zacharakis, Andrew.   III. Title.

   HG4027.7 .T55   2004
   658.15'92—dc22   2003026015

1 2 3 4 5 6 7 8 9 0   AGM/AGM 3 2 1 0 9 8 7 6 5 4

ISBN 0-07-141288-3

This book is printed on acid-free paper.

CONTENTS

INTRODUCTION

America is the land of entrepreneurial opportunity. The American Dream is one of doing better than your parents' generation in terms of education and standard of living. Entrepreneurship is often the path that leads people to that dream. The level of entrepreneurial activity in the United States leads the industrialized world. At any given point in time, over 10.6 percent of the adult population is pursuing an entrepreneurial venture or is the owner of a new business less than forty months old.* Yet this statistic is misleading because there are different types of entrepreneurship. Individuals such as Bill Gates (Microsoft), Arthur Blank (Home Depot), and Michael Dell (Dell Computer) have founded companies that not only became industry leaders but also changed the way we live and work. At the other end of the spectrum are the mom-and-pop owners of the local dry cleaner or pizza shop. Then there are all the entrepreneurial businesses in between. We describe these types of entrepreneurship as lifestyle, foundation firms, and high-potential ventures. What type of entrepreneur are you? More important, what type would you like to be?

Throughout our careers as entrepreneurs and educators we have seen many companies remain small even though they aspire to greater revenues and more wealth. In fact, the majority of all businesses operating in the United States today may be considered "small." Of these almost

*Global Entrepreneurship Monitor.

6 million firms, 4.8 million have less than one hundred employees (80 percent of all the firms in the country). Many of these small companies—which often employ less than ten people—do not lack for customer demand or entrepreneurial talent, but cannot break through the $1–$5 million sales barrier. Many others that grow to $20–$30 million get stuck. So why can't these companies break out and achieve their founder's vision? We have discovered that they make four key mistakes:

- **They don't think big enough** in terms of the opportunity and the team needed to exploit their opportunity.
- **They spend too much time and effort looking for the wrong resources from the wrong people.** Matching the right deal with the right investors brings smart money to a business and gives it the best chance to grow.
- **They don't instill entrepreneurial thinking in their team.** Many small firm entrepreneurs struggle mightily to learn the art of delegation. But we have found that some entrepreneurs don't make the link between growing the opportunity and growing the team. They tend to think they can expand their personal capacity to fill the needs of the opportunity. Often they end up tired and frustrated.
- **They don't think in terms of harvest strategy.** Most entrepreneurs start with a vision—a perspective on how they will create a great and prosperous company—but lose sight of it as they struggle to put out fires that arise every day.

The aim of this book is to help small business owners re-engage their entrepreneurial roots, guide them through problematic small business thinking, and help them create a wealth-building mentality. Entrepreneurship starts with opportunity, so we will ask you to reassess your company and your instincts. The reality is that many of the 4.8 million small businesses in the United States are undervalued because they have failed to reach their full potential.

CHAPTER 1

THE OPPORTUNITY
HAVE YOU CRAFTED A BUSINESS THAT WILL CREATE WEALTH?

"I was seldom able to see an opportunity, until it ceased to be one."
—MARK TWAIN

Think Big Enough

Our first job is to inspire you to "think big enough." Time and again the authors have observed the classic small business owner who is enslaved and wedded to the business. Extremely long workweeks of seventy, eighty, or even one hundred hours, and rare vacations, are often the rule rather than the exception. And these hard-working owners rarely build equity, other than in the real estate they may own for the business. The implication is clear: one of the big differences between the growth- and equity-minded entrepreneur and the traditional small business owner is that the entrepreneur thinks *bigger*. Longtime good friend Patricia Cloherty puts it this way: "It is critical to think big enough. If you want to start and build a company, you are going to end up exhausted. So you might as well think about creating a BIG company. At least you will end up exhausted and *rich*, not just exhausted!"

Pat has a wealth of experience as a venture capitalist and is past president of Patrioff & Company in New York City. She also served as the first female president of the National Venture Capital Association. In these capacities she has been a lead investor, board member, and creator of many highly successful businesses, many of which were acquired or achieved an initial public offering (IPO). Her theme of thinking bigger infuses this book. How can you engage in a "think big" process that takes you on a journey always treading the fine line between high ambitions and being totally out of your mind? How do you know whether the idea you are chasing is just another rainbow or indeed has a bona fide pot of gold at the end? The truth is that you can never know which side of the line you are on—and can stay on—until you try and until you undertake the journey.

Opportunity Through a Zoom Lens

As incomprehensible as thirty-nine rejections may be for many, the original proposal by founder Scott Cook to launch a new software company called Intuit was turned down by that many venture capital investors before it was funded! Thousands of similar examples illustrate just how complex, subtle, and situational (at the time, in the market space, compared with the investor's other alternatives, etc.) is the opportunity recognition process. If the brightest, most knowledgeable, and most sophisticated investors in the world miss opportunities like Intuit, we surely can conclude that the journey from small business to high value is illusive, contradictory, and perilous. Think of it as a sort of road trip through varied terrain and weather conditions. At times, the journey consists of full sunshine and straight, smooth superhighways, but it also has twisting, turning, narrow one-lane descents and ascents that lead to some of the most breathtaking views. Along the way you also will unexpectedly encounter tornadoes, dust storms, hurricanes, and volcanoes. All too often you seem to run out of gas without a service station in sight, and flat tires come when you least expect them. This is the entrepreneur's journey.

Transforming Caterpillars into Butterflies

This chapter is dedicated to making that journey friendlier by focusing a zoom lens on your small business. It shares the road maps and benchmarks used by successful entrepreneurs, venture capitalists, angels, and other private equity investors in their quest to transform the often-shapeless caterpillar of a small business into a spectacularly handsome butterfly of a high-value venture. These criteria constitute the core of their due diligence to ascertain the viability and profit potential of the business, and, therefore, the balance of risk and reward. This chapter will examine the role of ideas and pattern recognition in the creative process of entrepreneurship.

You will come to see the criteria used to identify higher-potential ventures as jumping-off points at this rarefied end of the opportunity continuum, rather than mere endpoints. One to ten out of one hundred entrepreneurs create ventures that emerge from the pack. Examined through a zoom lens, these ventures reveal a highly dynamic, constantly molding, shaping, and changing work of art in progress, rather than a product of a pat formula or one created by meeting certain conditions on a checklist. This highly organic and situational character of the entrepreneurial process underscores the criticality of determining *fit* and balancing *risk and reward*. As the authors have argued for decades: high-value businesses constantly evolve in the face of changing market demand and the nuances of the capital markets. It is in this shaping process that the best entrepreneurial leaders and investors add the greatest value to the enterprise, and creatively transform what may appear as a mundane caterpillar of a small business into a magnificent butterfly of a venture.

Small Company Realities

To begin with, it is useful to put some of the realities faced by Scott Cook and millions of others in perspective, as he is not alone in what he went through. Consider the following fundamental realities as normal and to be expected as you seek to convert your caterpillar of a company into a gorgeous butterfly:

New Ventures: Some Fundamental Realities
- Most companies are works in process and works of art.
- Your business plan is obsolete at the printer. (For example, Onset Venture Partners found that 91 percent of portfolio companies that followed their business plan *failed!*)

- Speed, adroitness of reflex, and adaptability are *crucial*.
- The key to succeeding is failing quickly and recouping quickly.
- Success is highly situational: time, space, context, and stakeholders.
- The best entrepreneurs specialize in making "new mistakes" only.
- You can last a lot longer and do more than you think if you avoid going it alone.

These realities are intended to convey the highly dynamic, at times chaotic, nature of this beast, and the fluctuating context within which most companies evolve. Such realities present so much room for the unexpected and the contradictory that it places a premium on thinking big enough and doing everything you can to make sure your company grows and creates value. Therefore, how can the aspiring entrepreneur think about this complex, even daunting, challenge?

The Circle of Ecstasy and the Food Chain for Ventures

What most small businesses do not know, but what is a way of life in the world of high-potential ventures, is what we will call the "circle of venture capital ecstasy" (Exhibit 1.1) and the "food chain for entrepreneurial ventures" (Exhibit 1.2). These concepts enable the entrepreneur to visualize clearly how the company building-investing-harvesting cycle works in practice. Understanding this cycle and the appetites of different suppliers in the capital markets food chain enables you to answer these questions: for *what* reason does this venture exist, and for *whom*? Knowing the answers has profound implications for fundraising, team building, and growing and harvesting the company—or settling into small business myopia that keeps you from thinking about anything but surviving each day.

In Exhibit 1.1 you can see that the key to creating a company with highest value begins with articulating your opportunity in the best technology and market space, which draws the best management teams. Speed and agility to move quickly in turn attracts the best investors, board members, and other mentors and advisors, who can truly add value to the venture.

Exhibit 1.2 captures the food chain concept, which will be discussed again in greater detail later in the book. Note that different players in the food chain have very different capacities and preferences for the kind of venture in which they want to invest. The vast majority of small-business people spend inordinate amounts of time chasing the wrong sources. One of our goals in this book is to provide a clear picture of what those criteria are and to grasp what "think big enough" means to the players in the food chain. This is a critical early step in avoiding time-wasting resource pursuits when there is simply a misfit from the outset. As one CEO put it, "There are so many investors out there that you could spend the rest of your career meeting with them and still not get to all of them."

Why waste time thinking too small and on ventures for which there is no appetite in the financial marketplace? Knowing how suppliers of

Exhibit 1.1 Circle of Venture Capital Ecstasy

Exhibit 1.2 The Capital Markets Food Chain for Entrepreneurial Ventures

Stage of Venture	R&D	Seed	Launch	High Growth
Company Enterprise Value at Stage	Less than $1 million	$1–$5 million	More than $1–$50 million	More than $100 million
Sources	Founders; high net-worth individuals; FFF*, SBIR†	FFF; angel funds; seed funds; SBIR	Venture capital series A, B, C . . . ‡; strategic partners; very high net-worth individuals; private equity	IPOs; strategic acquirers; private equity
Amount of Capital Invested	Up to $200,000	$10,000–$500,000	$500,000–$20 million	$10–$50 million +
Percentage Company Owned at IPO	10–25%	5–15%	40–60% by prior investors	15–25% by public
Share Price and Number§	$.01–$.50	$.50–$1.00	$1.00–$8.00 ±	$12–$18+
	1–5 million	1–3 million	5–10 million	3–5 million

* Friends, families, and fools
† Small Business Innovation Research, an N&F program
‡ Venture capital series A, B, C . . . (average size of round)
  A @ $5 million—start-up
  B @ $7.5 million—product development
  C @ $12 million—shipping product
Valuations vary markedly by industry (e.g., $2x^5$)
Valuations vary by region and VC cycle
§ At post-IPO

capital, and entrepreneurs, think about the opportunity creation and recognition process, their search and evaluation strategies, and what they look for is a key frame of reference.

When Is an Idea an Opportunity?

If an idea is not an opportunity, what is an opportunity? An opportunity has the qualities of being attractive, durable, and timely and is anchored in a product or service that creates or adds value for its buyer or end user.[1]

For an opportunity to have these qualities, the "window of opportunity" is opening and remains open long enough. Further, entry into a market with the right characteristics is feasible and the management team is able to achieve it. The venture has or is able to achieve a competitive advantage. Finally, the economics of the venture are rewarding and forgiving and allow significant profit and growth potential.

The most successful entrepreneurs, venture capitalists, and private investors are opportunity focused; that is, they are obsessed with what customers and the marketplace want and do not lose sight of this.

The Real World

Great companies are built using ideas and entrepreneurial creativity. Yet while the metaphor of a carpenter or mason at work is useful, in reality the process is more like the collision of particles in the process of a nuclear reaction, or like the spawning of hurricanes over the ocean. Ideas interact with real-world conditions and entrepreneurial vision at a point in time. The product of this interaction is an opportunity around which a new venture can be created. Small businesses sometimes lose sight of this entrepreneurial chemistry and stay small in an attempt to control their environment. In reality, the business environment in which an entrepreneur launches his or her venture is usually fixed and cannot be altered significantly.

Spawners and Drivers of Opportunities

In a free enterprise system, *opportunities* are spawned when there are changing circumstances, chaos, confusion, inconsistencies, lags or leads, knowledge and information gaps, and a variety of other vacuums in an industry or market.

Changes in the business environment and, therefore, anticipation of these changes are so critical in entrepreneurship that constant vigilance for changes is a valuable habit. It is thus that an entrepreneur with credibility, creativity, and decisiveness can seize an opportunity while others study it.

Opportunities are situational. Some conditions under which opportunities are spawned are entirely idiosyncratic, while at other times they are generalizable and can be applied to other industries, products, or services. In this way, cross-association can trigger in the entrepreneurial mind the crude recognition of existing or impending opportunities. It is often assumed that a marketplace dominated by large, multibillion-dollar players is impenetrable by smaller, entrepreneurial companies. After all, how can you possibly compete with entrenched, resource-rich, established companies? The opposite can be true for several reasons. It can take years or more for a large company to change its strategy, and even longer to implement it—often ten years or more to change the culture enough to operate differently. For a new or small company, ten or more years is forever. When Cellular One was launched in Boston, giant NYNEX was the sole competitor. From all estimates NYNEX built twice as many towers (at $400,000 each) and spent two to three times as much on advertising and marketing, in addition to having a larger head count. Yet Cellular One grew from scratch to $100 million in sales in five years and won three times as many customers as NYNEX. What made this substantial difference? It was an entrepreneurial management team at Cellular One.

Some of the most exciting opportunities have actually come from fields the conventional wisdom said are the domain of big business: technological innovation. The performance of smaller firms in technological innovation is remarkable—95 percent of the radical innovations since World War II have come from new and small firms, not the giants. In fact, another study from the National Science Foundation found that smaller firms generated twenty-four times as many innovations per research and development dollar versus firms with ten thousand or more employees.[2]

There are many exciting opportunities in plain vanilla businesses that might never get the attention of venture capital investors. The revolution in microcomputers, management information systems (MIS), and computer networking had a profound impact on a number of businesses that had changed little in decades. The used-auto-wreck and used-auto-parts business is one good example. The team at Pintendre Auto, Inc., saw a new opportunity in this field by applying the latest computer and information technology to a traditional business that had relied on crude, manual methods to track inventory and find parts for customers.[3] In just three years, they built a business with $16 million in sales.

Technology and regulatory changes have profoundly altered and will continue to revise the way we conceive of opportunities. Cable television with its hundreds of channels came of age in the 1990s and brought with it new opportunities in the sale and distribution of goods from infomercials to shopping networks to pay-per-view. The Internet has created an even more diverse set of opportunities in sales and distribution, most notably Amazon.com, Priceline, and eBay.

Consider the following examples of vacuums in which opportunities are spawned:

- Deregulation of telecommunications and the airlines led to the formation of tens of thousands of new firms in the 1980s, including Cellular One (now Cingular) and Federal Express.
- Microcomputer hardware in the early 1980s far outpaced the development of software. The industry, however, was highly dependent on software, leading to aggressive efforts by IBM, Apple, and others to encourage software entrepreneurs to close this gap. The lessons learned from this experienced translated to the PDA industry, which is expected to grow to $17 billion by 2007. Thousands of software products have been developed, and PDA hardware is rapidly evolving to integrate with cellular hardware and technology.

- Many opportunities exist in fragmented, traditional industries that may have a craft or mom-and-pop character and where there is little appreciation or know-how in marketing and finance. Such possibilities can range from fishing lodges, inns, and hotels (Holiday Inn Express) to cleaners/laundries (Zoots), hardware stores (Home Depot), pharmacies (CVS), waste management plants (Waste Managment Corp.), flower shops (Kabloom), preschool education (KinderCare), and auto repairs (Jiffy Lube). But no industry faces more challenges than music. There is a proliferation of channels through which consumers access music. New carriers are coming to market DVD Audio and Super Audio CD and, in the longer term, flash memory. Control software (DRM, encryption, compression, etc.) and access technologies (broadband Internet, mobile computing) are a threat to old thinkers and an opportunity to entrepreneurs. The value chain is being violently disrupted. Consider the possibilities (probabilities!): virtual record labels, online radio, digital downloads, file sharing, and subscription services are just a few of the growing new business models.

- In our service-dominated economy (where 70 percent of businesses are service businesses, versus 30 percent just twenty-five years ago), customer service, rather than the product itself, can be the critical success factor. The Carlson Marketing Group's[4] annual brand survey found that brand loyalty has decreased by 25 percent in 2003. Yet the same survey found that those organizations that provided a good experience for their customers over various channels had loyalty levels 33 percent higher than the norm. Can you think of your last "wow" experience with exceptional customer service?

- Sometimes existing competitors cannot, or will not, increase capacity as the market is moving. For example, in the late 1970s, some steel firms had a ninety-week delivery lag, with the price to be determined, and foreign competitors certainly took notice. The tremendous shift to offshore manufacturing of labor-intensive and transportation-intensive products (such as computer-related and microprocessor-drive consumer products) in Asia, Eastern Europe, and Mexico is another excellent example.

- In a wide variety of industries, entrepreneurs sometimes find that they are the only ones who can perform. Such fields as consulting, software design, financial services, process engineering, and technical and medical products and services abound with examples of know-how monopolies. Sometimes a management team is simply the best in an industry and irreplaceable in the near term, just as is seen with great coaches with winning records.

Exhibit 1.3 summarizes the major types of discontinuities, asymmetries, and changes that can result in high-potential opportunities. Creating such changes, by technical innovation (PCs, wireless telecommunications, Internet servers, software), influencing and creating the new rules of the game (airlines, telecommunications, financial services and banking, medical products), and anticipating the various impacts of such changes is central to the opportunity recognition process.

Search for Sea Changes

Probably the most profound but simple criterion for the highest potential ventures came from famed venture capitalist Arthur Rock: "We look for ideas that will change the way people live or work." As a lead investor in Apple Computer and a host of other world-class start-ups, he knows of what he speaks. The best place to start in a macro sense is to identify significant sea changes that are occurring, or that will occur. Think of the profound impact that personal computing, biotechnology, and the Internet have had on the past generation. The great new ventures of the next generation will come about by the same process and will define these next great sea changes. Exhibit 1.4 summarizes some categories for thinking about such changes. These include technology, market and societal shifts, and even opportunities spawned from the excesses produced by the Internet boom. Certainly, Moore's Law (that the computing power of a chip doubles every eighteen months) has been a gigantic driver of much of our technological revolution over the past thirty years. New breakthroughs in gene mapping and cloning, biotech-

Exhibit 1.3 Opportunity Spawners and Drivers

Root of Change/ Chaos/Discontinuity	Opportunity Creation
Regulatory changes	Cellular, airlines, insurance, radio and television, telecommunications, medical, pension fund management, financial services, banking, tax and SEC laws
Tenfold change in ten years or less	Moore's Law—computer chips double productivity every eighteen months; financial services; private equity, consulting, Internet, biotech, information age, publishing
Reconstruction of value chain and channels of distribution	Superstores: Staples, Home Depot; all publishing; autos; Internet sales and distribution of all services
Proprietary or contractual advantage	Technological innovation; patent, license, contract, franchise, copyrights, distributorship
Existing management/investors burned out/undermanaged	Turnaround, new capital structure, new breakeven, new free cash flow, new team, new strategy; owners' desires for liquidity, exit; telecom, waste management service, retail businesses
Entrepreneurial leadership	New vision and strategy, new team = secret weapon; organization thinks and acts like owners
Market leaders are customer obsessed or customer blind	New, small customers are low priority or ignored; hard disk drives, paper, chemicals, mainframes, centralized data processing, desktop computers, corporate venturing, office superstores, automobiles, software, most services
Imperfect information and markets	Intangibles, art, private equity and venture capital, antiques
Disruptive technologies and exogenous events	Internet services, wireless telecommunications, LED lighting, handheld personal communications devices; September 11, 2001

nology, nanotechnology, and changes brought about by the World Wide Web will continue to create huge opportunities for the next generation. Beyond the macro view of sea changes, how can one think about opportunities in a more practical, less abstract sense? What are some parameters of business/revenue models that increase the odds of thinking big enough and that therefore appeal to the food chain?

Exhibit 1.4 Ideas Versus Opportunities: Search for Sea Changes

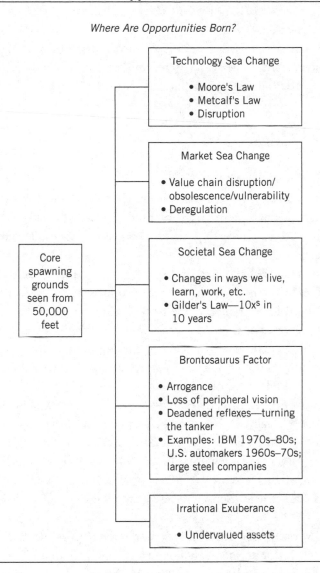

Where Are Opportunities Born?

Desirable Business/Revenue Model Metrics
==

We will emphasize time and again that happiness is a positive cash flow!
Many small businesses use a checkbook mentality and forget to exam-

ine and reexamine the free cash flow characteristic of their business. What were the compelling reasons you first launched your venture? How has the world and your business changed since then? Is the opportunity as exciting as it used to be? How can you shape your business to react to the current status of the opportunity to make it more exciting (read "more exciting" as "increasing cash flow")?

The Role of Ideas

Ideas as Tools

It is worth emphasizing again that a good idea is nothing more than a tool in the hands of an entrepreneur. Finding a good idea is the first step in the task of converting an entrepreneur's creativity into an opportunity.

The importance of the idea is most often overrated, usually at the expense of underemphasizing the need for products or services, or both, which can be sold in enough quantity to real customers. Most small business owners realize this and have real-time market intelligence that gives them a competitive advantage. But they sometimes lack the perspective on how their knowledge of the products and services translates into scale. We'll talk about that later.

Further, the new business that simply bursts from a flash of brilliance is rare. What is usually necessary is a series of trial-and-error iterations, or repetitions, before a crude and promising product or service fits with what the customer is really willing to pay for. If you have experienced this as a small business owner it's perfectly normal and tends to strengthen your mettle. Consider these examples:

- When 3M chemist Spence Silver invented a new adhesive that would not dry or permanently bond to things, he had no idea what to do with it. It wasn't until another 3M chemist named Arthur Fry needed a bookmark for his choir book that the idea for applying the glue to small pieces of paper was tried, and Post-it Notes were born.[5]

- Michael Healy founded PC Build in 1993 as a computer "kit" company for the do-it-yourselfer and computer camp industry. By 2003 the company had become Technology Enterprise Network Corporation (TENCorp), the largest computer network installer for public schools in New England.[6]
- William Steere, CEO of Pfizer, described the discovery of Viagra, the fastest-selling drug in history, as having "a certain serendipity" behind it. The drug was originally developed by Pfizer to treat angina—its real "potency" was discovered as a side effect.[7]

The Great Mousetrap Fallacy

Perhaps no one did a greater disservice to generations of would-be entrepreneurs than Ralph Waldo Emerson in his oft-quoted line: "If a man can make a better mousetrap than his neighbor, though he builds his house in the woods the world will make a beaten path to his door."

What can be called the great mousetrap fallacy was thus spawned. Indeed, it is often assumed that success is possible if an entrepreneur can just come up with a new idea. In today's changing world, if the idea has anything to do with technology, success is certain—or so it would seem.

The truth of the matter is that ideas are inert and, for all practical purposes, worthless. Further, the flow of ideas is really quite phenomenal. Venture capital investors during the investing boom of the late 1990s, for instance, received as many as two hundred proposals and business plans each month. Only 2 or 3 percent of these actually received financing.

Yet the fallacy persists despite the lessons of practical experience noted long ago in O. B. Winters's insightful reply to Emerson: "The manufacturer who waits for the world to beat a path to his door is a great optimist. But the manufacturer who shows this 'mousetrap' to the world keeps the smoke coming out his chimney."

The great mousetrap fallacy traps many small-business people. They have a great idea and what seems like a sound business model. Often scale and growth is a channel problem that needs sophisticated attention.

Contributors to the Fallacy

One cannot blame it all on Ralph Waldo Emerson. There are several reasons for the perpetuation of the fallacy. One is the portrayal in over-simplified accounts of the ease and genius with which such ventures as Intel, Microsoft, and eBay made their founders wealthy. Unfortunately, these exceptions do not provide a useful rule to guide small business owners.

Another is that inventors seem particularly prone to mousetrap myopia. Perhaps, like Emerson, they are substantially sheltered in view-point and experience from the tough, competitive realities of the business world. Consequently, they may underestimate, if not seriously downgrade, the importance of what it takes to make a successful small business grow. Frankly, inventing and brainstorming may be a lot more fun than the careful diligent observation, investigation, and nurturing of customers that are often required to sell a product or service. Contributing also to the great mousetrap fallacy is the tremendous psychological ownership attached to an invention or, after, to a new product. This is different from an attachment to a business. While an intense level of psychological ownership and involvement is certainly a prerequisite for creating a new business, the fatal flaw in attachment to an invention or product is the narrowness of its focus. The focal point needs to be the building of the business, rather than just one aspect of the idea.

Another source of mousetrap fallacy myopia lies in a technical and scientific orientation—that is, a desire to do it better. A good illustration of this is the experience of a Canadian entrepreneur who founded, with his brother, a company to manufacture truck seats. The entrepreneur's brother had developed a new seat for trucks that was a definite improvement over other seats. The entrepreneur knew he could profitably sell the seat his brother had designed, and they did so. When they needed more manufacturing capacity, the designer was more interested in making further improvements rather than manufacturing more of the first seat. The first brother stated: "If I had listened to him, we probably would be a small custom shop today, or out of business. Instead, we concentrated on making seats that would sell at a profit, rather than just making a better and better seat. Our company has several million dollars of sales today and is profitable."

Related to "doing it better" is the idea of doing it first. It should be noted that having the best idea first is by no means a guarantee of success. Just ask the creators of the first spreadsheet software, VisiCalc, what being first did for them: sometimes the first ones merely prove to the competition that a market exists to be snared. Therefore, unless having the best idea also includes the capacity to preempt other competitors by capturing a significant share of the market or by erecting insurmountable barriers to entry, first does not necessarily mean most viable. Mark Twain once said, "The best swordsman in the world does not need to fear the second best swordsman in the world, but rather the man ignorant of swords but knowledgeable about gun powder."

Pattern Recognition

The Experience Factor: The Competitive Weapon You Shouldn't Keep Secret

Since ideas are building tools, one cannot build a successful business without them, as one could not build a house without a hammer. In this regard, using your experience is vital in evaluating ideas and growing your business. Those with experience have been there before, know where a lot of landmines are, and can better map the route to a successful future. The problem is that some small business entrepreneurs don't leverage their experience. Others do.

Time after time we've identified experienced entrepreneurs who exhibit an ability to recognize quickly a pattern—and an opportunity—while it is still taking shape. The late Herbert Simon, Nobel laureate and Richard King Mellon University Professor of Computer Science and Psychology at Carnegie-Mellon University, wrote extensively about pattern recognition. He described a creative process that is not simply logical, linear, and additive but intuitive and inductive as well. It involves the creative linking, or cross-association, of two or more in-depth "chunks" of experience, know-how, and contacts.[8] Simon contended that it takes ten years or more for people to accumulate what he called the "50,000 chunks" of experience that enable them to be highly creative and recognize patterns—familiar circumstances that can be translated from one place to another. We have found that growing a company continually adds "chunks of knowledge" on top of these 50,000 to shape the opportunity.

Thus, the process of sorting through ideas and recognizing a pattern can also be compared to the process of fitting pieces into a three-dimensional jigsaw puzzle. It is impossible to assemble such a puzzle by looking at it as a whole unit. Rather, one needs to see the relationships between the pieces, and be able to fit together some that are seemingly unrelated before the whole is visible.

Consider the following examples of the common thread of pattern recognition and creating new businesses by linking knowledge in one field or marketplace with quite different technical, business, or market know-how:

- In 1973, Thomas Stemberg worked for Star Market in Boston where he became known for launching the first line of low-priced generic foods. Twelve years later he applied the same low-cost, large volume supermarket business model to office supplies. The result was Staples, the first office superstore and today a multibillion-dollar company.[9]
- During travel throughout Europe, the eventual founders of Crate & Barrel frequently saw stylish and innovative products for the kitchen and home that were not available in the United States. When they returned home, they established Crate & Barrel to offer these products for which market research had, in a sense, already been done. In Crate & Barrel, the knowledge of consumer buying habits in one geographical region, Europe, was transferred successfully to another, the United States.

Enhancing Creative Thinking

The creative thinking described above is of great value in recognizing and shaping opportunities, which is essential to growing a business. The notion that creativity can be learned or enhanced holds important implications for entrepreneurs who need to be creative in their thinking.

Most people can certainly spot creative flair. Children seem to have it, but many seem to lose it. Several studies suggest that creativity actually peaks around the first grade, because a person's life tends to become increasingly structured and defined by others and by institutions. Further, the development in school of intellectual discipline and rigor takes on greater importance than during the formative years, and most of our education beyond grade school stresses a logical, rational mode of orderly reasoning and thinking. Finally, social pressures may tend to be a taming influence on creativity.

There is evidence that one can enhance creative thinking in later years. Eureka! Ranch was founded on the principle that creativity is inherent in most people and can be unleashed by freeing them from convention (eurekaranch.com). Oftentimes, executives will be doused with water as they step out of their vehicles onto the ranch.

Approaches to Unleashing Creativity

Many scholars have focused on the creativity process. For instance, Michael Gordon stressed the importance of creativity and the need for brainstorming in a recent presentation on the elements of personal power. He suggested that following these ten brainstorming rules can enhance creative visualization:*

1. Define your purpose
2. Choose participants
3. Choose a facilitator
4. Brainstorm spontaneously, copiously
5. No criticisms, no negatives
6. Record ideas in full view
7. Invent to the "void"
8. Resist becoming committed to one idea
9. Identify the most promising ideas
10. Refine and prioritize

*Special thanks to Dr. Michael Gordon, lecturer at Babson College, who granted permission to use these brainstorming rules, which he developed several years ago and uses in his educational and professional presentations.

Team Creativity

Teams of people can generate creativity that may not exist in a single individual. Continually, the creativity of a team of people is impressive, and better creative solutions to problems evolving from the collective interaction of a small group of people have been observed.

This can be problematic for the small business owner who has not built a working team or whose team is intimidated by the founder. Small business owners need to look in the mirror and make an honest assessment of the team. Food-processing entrepreneur Eric Johnson says of his company Baldwin Richardson Foods: "We began to grow in earnest when we decided that we would be a team of 'A' players. 'A' players are people who set high goals and collaborate to achieve them. You have to remember, zero is not the lowest addition a player can add to a team. Some folks are negative contributors. They become especially negative when they drag other people into mediocre performance."[10]

Big Opportunities with Little Capital

Ironically, successful entrepreneurs like Howard Head attribute their success to the discipline of *limited capital resources*. Thus, in the early 1990s, many entrepreneurs learned the key to success is in the art of bootstrapping, which, says Amar Bhide, "in a startup is like zero inventory in a just-in-time system: it reveals hidden problems and forces the company to solve them."[11] Consider the following:

- The 2003 *Inc.* 500 study revealed that 61 percent of the businesses had been launched with $50,000 or less. Further, the primary source of capital was, overwhelmingly, personal savings (80 percent) rather than outside investors with deep pockets.[12]
- In the 1930s, Josephine Esther Mentzer assisted her uncle by selling skin care balm and quickly created her own products with a $100 initial investment. After convincing the department stores rather than the drugstores to carry her products, Estée Lauder was on its way to a $4 billion corporation.[13]

- Putting their talents (cartooning and finance) together, Walt and Roy Disney moved to California and in 1923 started their own film studio—with $290. By mid-2001, the Walt Disney Co. had a market capitalization exceeding $40 billion.[14]
- While working for a Chicago insurance company, a twenty-four-year-old sent out twenty thousand inquiries for a black newsletter. With three thousand positive responses and $500, John Harold Johnson published *Jet* for the first time in 1942. In the 1990s, Johnson Publishing had expanded to print various other magazines, including *Ebony*.[15]
- Nicholas Graham, also twenty-four, went to a local fabric store, picked out some patterns, and made $100 worth of ties. After selling the ties to specialty shops, Graham was approached by Macy's to use his patterns on men's underwear. So Joe Boxer Corporation was born, with sales exceeding $1 million after just eighteen months.[16]
- Boo.com, an Internet fashion start-up, failed six months after launching with a $200 million war chest. It reportedly had had no project plan for months. The *New York Times* quoted a former staff member as claiming that "employees routinely flew first class and stayed in five-star hotels." *The Industry Standard* reported that a Boo founder realized, much too late, that the business had needed "a strong financial controller."[17]

Real Time

Opportunities exist or are created in real time and have what we call a window of opportunity. The small business must seize an opportunity when the window is open and remains open long enough to achieve required market returns.

Exhibit 1.5 illustrates a window of opportunity for a generalized market. Markets grow at different rates over time. As a market quickly becomes larger, more and more opportunities are possible. But as the market becomes larger and more established, conditions are not as favorable. Thus, at the point where a market starts to become sufficiently large and structured (e.g., at five years in Exhibit 1.5), the win-

Exhibit 1.5 Changes in the Placement of the Window of Opportunity

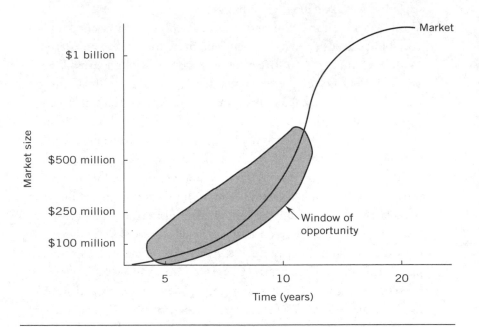

dow opens; the window begins to close as the market matures (e.g., at twelve to thirteen years in the exhibit).

The curve shown describes the rapid growth pattern typical of such new industries as microcomputers and software, cell phones, quick oil changes, and biotechnology. For example, in the cellular car phone industry, most major cities began service between 1983 and 1984 for the very first time. By 2002 the industry had grown to $80 billion, expanding beyond voice to include text, wireless gaming, digital photography, and downloaded custom ringing. But "number portability" (switching mobile phone companies without having to change your phone number) could mean as many as 40 percent of current users will change carriers.[18]

Finally, in considering the window of opportunity, the duration the window will be open is important. It takes a considerable length of time to determine whether a new venture is a success or a failure. And, if it is to be a success, the benefits of that success need to be harvested.

Exhibit 1.6 illustrates how the winners gain investment as the window opens and closes and opens again over time. Another way to think of the process of creating and seizing an opportunity in real time is to think of it as a process of selecting objects (opportunities) from a conveyor belt moving through an open window, the window of opportunity. The speed of the conveyor belt changes and the window through

Exhibit 1.6 Lemons and Pearls

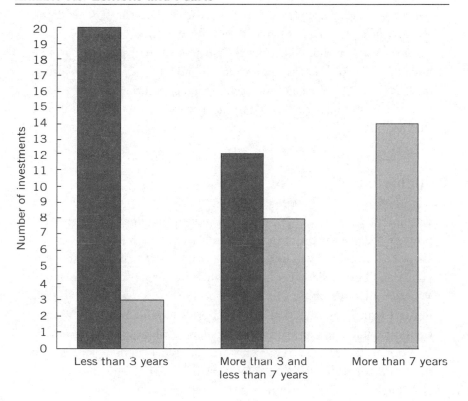

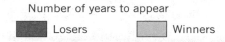

which it moves is constantly opening and closing. This represents the volatile nature of the marketplace and the importance of timing. For an opportunity to be created and seized, it needs to be selected from the conveyor belt before the window closes.

The ability to recognize a potential opportunity when it appears and the sense of timing to seize that opportunity as the window is opening, rather than slamming shut, is critical. This is vividly illustrated by several quotations from very famous innovators. In 1977 Ken Olsen, president and founder of Digital Equipment Corporation, said: "There is no reason for any individual to have a computer in their home." Nor is it so easy for even the world's leading experts to predict just which innovative ideas and concepts for new business will evolve into the major industries of tomorrow. In 1901, two years before the famous flight, Wilbert Wright said, "Man will not fly for fifty years." In 1910, Thomas Edison said, "The nickel-iron battery will put the gasoline buggy . . . out of existence in no time." And in 1932, Albert Einstein made it clear: "There is not the slightest indication that nuclear energy will ever be obtainable. It would mean that the atom would have to be shattered at will."

Conclusion

Entrepreneurship is an opportunity to solve problems. The bigger the problem the greater the chance a venture will be high potential. In this chapter we implored you to think big enough and examine the scope of your small business and begin to visualize the size of the opportunity. When you form a bigger vision, the world of entrepreneurship, clearly illustrated in Exhibits 1.1 and 1.2, will open to you. You'll gain access to the capital markets, strategic partners, and growing customers. Remember, the great entrepreneurs are action oriented. Their vision is focused through the lens of desirable business and revenue model metrics. They obsessively analyze and shape their vision into products and services that anchor the opportunity. In Chapter 1 we spent a lot of time discussing the characteristics of a high-potential venture. Many small-business people have spent their lives embedding an intuitive understanding of their industry and business. As we continue our discussion of analyzing your business's potential and gaining resources to achieve that potential, we hope you will go from the intuitive to the intentional.

Notes

1. See Jeffry A. Timmons, *New Business Opportunities* (Acton, MA: Brick House Publishing, 1989).

2. Richard Leifer, Lois S. Peters, Christopher McDermott, Gina C. O'Connor, Mark Rice, and Robert Veryzer, *Radical Innovation* (Harvard Business School Press, 2000).

3. Barrie McKenna, "More than the Sum of Its Parts," *The Globe and Mail*, Feb. 23, 1993, p. B24.

4. carlsoncanada.com.

5. P. R. Nayak and J. M. Ketterman, *Breakthroughs: How the Vision and Drive of Innovators in Sixteen Companies Created Commercial Breakthroughs That Swept the World*, Chapter 3 (New York: Rawson Associates, 1986).

6. TenCorp.com.

7. Tracy Corrigan. "Far More than the Viagra Company: Essential Guide to William Steere," *The Financial Times* (*London*), Aug. 31, 1998, p. 7.

8. Herbet A. Simon, "What We Know About the Creative Process," in *Frontiers in Creative and Innovative Management*, ed. R. L. Kuhn (Cambridge, MA: Ballinger Publishing Co., 1985), pp. 3–20.

9. Joseph Pereira, "Focus, Drive and an Eye for Discounts: Staples of Stemberg's Business Success," *Wall Street Journal*, Sept. 6, 1996, p. A9B (Eastern edition).

10. In an interview conducted at Baldwin Richardson offices on July 10, 2003.

11. Amar Bhide, "Bootstrap Finance," *Harvard Business Review*, Nov.–Dec. 1992, p. 112.

12. *Inc.*, Oct. 2003.

13. Teri Lammers and Annie Longsworth, "Guess Who? Ten Big-Timers Launched from Scratch," *Inc.*, Sept. 1991, p. 69.

14. Financial data from Dow Jones Interactive: djnr.com.

15. Ibid.

16. Robert A. Mamis, "The Secrets of Bootstrapping," *Inc.*, Sept. 1991, p. 54.

17. shorewalker.com/design/design104.html (first published May 29, 2000).

18. "Mobile Number Portability: A Mixed Blessing," datamonitor.com (Aug. 2002).

CHAPTER 2

ASSESSING YOUR COMPANY'S POTENTIAL

*"Know yourself and know the enemy . . . and you will know the
outcome of the battle before it starts."*

—TSUN ZSU

The iterative process of assessing and *reassessing* the fit among the central driving forces in the creation of a new venture are vital to the growth of a business. Of utmost importance when talking about the growth potential of a small business is the fit of the lead entrepreneur and the management team with an opportunity. Good opportunities are both desirable to and attainable by those on the team using available resources.

In order to understand how the entrepreneurial vision relates to the analytical framework, it may be useful to look at an opportunity as a three-dimensional relief map with its valleys, mountains, and so on, all represented. Each opportunity has three or four critical factors (e.g., proprietary license, patented innovation, sole distribution rights, an all-star management team, breakthrough technology). These elements pop out at the observer; they indicate huge possibilities where others might see obstacles. Thus, it is easy to see why thousands of exceptional opportunities will fit with a wide variety of entrepreneurs but not fall neatly into the framework outlined in Exhibit 2.1.

Exhibit 2.1 Criteria for Evaluating Venture Opportunities

Criteria	Attractiveness	
	Highest Potential	**Lowest Potential**
Industry and Market		
Market:	Changes way people live and work	Incremental improvement only
	Market driven; identified; recurring revenue niche	Unfocused; one-time revenue
Customers	Reachable; purchase orders	Loyal to others or unreachable
User benefits	Less than one-year payback	Three years plus payback
Value added	High; advance payments	Low; minimal impact on market
Product life	Durable	Perishable
Market structure	Imperfect, fragmented competition or emerging industry	Highly concentrated or mature or declining industry
Market size	$100+ million to $1 billion sales potential	Unknown, less than $20 million or multibillion sales
Growth rate	Growth at 30–50% or more	Contracting or less than 10%
Market capacity	At or near full capacity	Under capacity
Market share attainable (Year 5)	20% or more; leader	Less than 5%
Cost Structure	Low-cost provider; cost advantages	Declining cost

Economics

Time to breakeven/positive cash flow	Less than 1½–2 years	More than 4 years
ROI potential	25% or more per year	Less than 15–20%
Capital requirement	Low to moderate; fundable	Very high; unfundable
Internal rate of return potential	25% or more per year	Less than 15% per year
Free cash flow characteristics:	Favorable; sustainable; 20–30% or more of sales	Less than 10% of sales
Sales growth	Moderate to high +15% to +20%	Less than 10%
Asset intensity	Low/sales $	High
Spontaneous working capital	Low, incremental requirements	High requirements
R&D/capital expenditures	Low requirements	High requirements
Gross margins	Exceeding 40% and durable	Under 20%
After-tax profits	High; greater than 10%; durable	Low
Time to break-even profit and loss	Less than two years; breakeven not creeping	Greater than four years; breakeven creeping up

Harvest Issues

Value-added potential	High strategic value	Low strategic value
Valuation multiples and comparables	Price/earnings = $20 + x_\$$; $8\text{–}10 + x_\$$	Price/earnings $\leq 5x$, EBIT $\leq 3\text{–}4x$;
	EBIT $1.5\text{–}2 + x_\$$, revenue: free cash flow $8\text{–}10 + x_\$$	revenue $\leq .4$

(continued)

Exhibit 2.1 Criteria for Evaluating Venture Opportunities (continued)

Criteria	Highest Potential	Lowest Potential
Exit mechanism and strategy	Present or envisioned options	Undefined; illiquid investment
Capital market content	Favorable valuations, timing, capital available; realizable liquidity	Unfavorable; credit crunch
Competitive Advantage Issues		
Fixed and variable costs	Lowest; high operating leverage	Highest
Control over costs, prices, and distribution	Moderate to strong	Weak
Barriers to entry		
Proprietary protection	Have or can gain	None
Response/lead time	Competition slow or napping	Unable to gain edge
Legal, contractual advantage	Proprietary or exclusivity	None
Contracts and networks	Well-developed; accessible	Crude; limited
Key people	Top talent; an A team	B or C team
Management Team		
Entrepreneurial team	All-star combination; free agents	Weak or solo entrepreneur
Industry and technical experience	Top of the field; super track record	Underdeveloped
Integrity	Highest standards	Questionable
Intellectual honesty	Know what they do not know	Do not want to know what they do not know
Fatal-Flaw Issue	Nonexistent	One or more

Personal Criteria

Goals and fit	Getting what you want, but wanting what you get	Surprises, as in *The Crying Game*
Upside/downside issues	Attainable success/limited risks	Linear; on same continuum
Opportunity costs	Acceptable cuts in salary, etc.	Comfortable with status quo
Desirability	Fits with lifestyle	Simply pursuing big money
Risk/reward tolerance	Calculated risk; low risk/reward ratio	Risk averse or gambler
Stress tolerance	Thrives under pressure	Cracks under pressure

Strategic Differentiation

Degree of fit	High	Low
Team	Best in class; excellent free agents	B team; no free agents
Service management	Superior service concept	Perceived as unimportant
Timing	Rowing with the tide	Rowing against the tide
Technology	Groundbreaking; one of a kind	Many substitutes or competitors
Flexibility	Able to adapt; commit and decommit quickly	Slow; stubborn
Opportunity orientation	Always searching for opportunities	Operating in a vacuum; napping
Pricing	At or near leader	Undercut competitor; low prices
Distribution channels	Accessible; networks in place	Unknown; inaccessible
Room for error	Forgiving strategy	Unforgiving, rigid strategy

How Attractive Might Your Company Become?

We have spent many years building companies and counseling others to do the same. And we have come to recognize that growing a company is a natural extension of new venture creation. Entrepreneurship doesn't end with the creation of a venture. Indeed it is the growth and flourishing of a firm that fulfills the entrepreneurial promise.

The criterion used for assessing firm growth mirrors the opportunity screening process. However, there is a key difference. You have deep knowledge of the industry and the much-textured application of that knowledge. The problem lies in organizing that information and taking action based on your strategic vision!

The venture growth assessment framework (Exhibit 2.2) is not a "scorecard." Don't expect to tally a value at the end that will present a go/no-go decision. Rather, allow it to help you organize the intellectual capital owned within your firm and share it with trusted advisors and key partners. Once you have created the knowledge platform, act on it.

Assessing Your Deal

Opportunity Focus

"Screening" your company, or understanding if it has high value-creating potential, is a process that should not begin with strategy (which derives from the nature of the opportunity), nor with financial and spreadsheet analysis (which flow from the former), nor with estimations of how much the company is worth and who will own what shares.[1]

These starting points, and others, usually place the cart before the horse. Perhaps the best evidence of this phenomenon comes from the thousands of dot-com investments that turned sour in 2000, that were investor driven and not value focused. A good number of small business owners who try to grow run out of cash at a faster rate than they bring in customers and profitable sales.

Over the years, those with experience in business and in specific market areas have developed rules of thumb to guide them in screening opportunities. For example, during the initial stages of the irrational exuberance about the dot-com phenomenon, numbers of "clicks"

Exhibit 2.2 Venture Growth Assessment

Criteria	Attractiveness	
	Highest Potential	Lowest Potential
Industry and Market		
Market:	Changes way people live and work; Market driven; identified; recurring revenue niche	Incremental improvement only; Unfocused; one-time revenue
Customers	Reachable; we have long-term, loyal customers	Loyal to others or a struggle to reach
User benefits	Less than one-year payback	More than three-year payback
Value added	High; advance payments	Low; minimal impact on market
Product life	Durable	Perishable
Market structure	Imperfect, fragmented competition or emerging industry	Highly concentrated, mature, or declining industry
Market size	$100+ million to $1 billion	Unknown, less than $20 million or multibillion
Growth rate	Growth at 30–50% or more in the last three years	Contracting or less than 10% growth over the last three years (and we're not getting our share)
Market capacity	At or near full capacity; Under capacity	Need for company growth; Plenty of companies looking for new business
Market share attainable (Year 5)	No identifiable leader	Less than 5%
Cost structure	Low-cost provider; cost advantages	Declining cost . . . this is becoming a commodity

(continued)

Exhibit 2.2 Venture Growth Assessment (continued)

Criteria	Highest Potential	Lowest Potential
Economics		
Breakeven/positive cash flow	Consistent free cash flow	Highly cyclical with years of positive and years of negative cash flow
ROI potential	25% or more per year	Less than 10%
Capital requirement	Low to moderate; fundable	Very high; always struggling to fund or can't find funding
Internal rate of return potential	25% or more per year	Less than 15% per year
Free cash flow characteristics:	Favorable; sustainable; 20–30% or more of sales	Less than 10% of sales
Sales growth	Moderate to high: +15% to +20%	Less than 10%
Asset intensity	Low/sales $	High/sales $
Spontaneous working capital	Low, incremental requirements	High requirements
R&D/capital expenditures	Low requirements	High requirements
Gross margins	Exceeding 40%; durable	Under 20% or declining
After-tax profits	High; greater than 10%; durable	Low; 0–10%, and unstable
Break-even profit and loss	Breakeven not creeping up	Breakeven creeping up
Harvest Issues		
Value-added potential	High strategic value	Low strategic value
Valuation multiples and comparables	Price/earnings = $20 + x_s$; $8\text{–}10 + x_s$, EBIT $1.5\text{–}2 + x_s$, revenue: free cash flow $8\text{–}10 + x_s$	Price/earnings $\leq 5x$, EBIT $\leq 3\text{–}4x$; revenue $\leq .4$

Exit mechanism and strategy	I can name the companies that should buy us.	Undefined; illiquid investment
Capital market content	Favorable valuations, timing, capital available; realizable liquidity	Unfavorable; credit crunch

Competitive Advantage Issues

Fixed and variable costs	Lowest; high operating leverage	Highest
Control over costs, prices, and distribution	Moderate to strong	Weak
Barriers to entry:		
Proprietary protection	Have or can gain	None
Response/lead time	Competition slow or napping	Unable to gain edge
Legal, contractual advantage	Proprietary or exclusivity	None
Contracts and networks	Well-developed; reliable	Crude; limited, unreliable
Key people	Top talent: an A team	B or C team

Management Team

Entrepreneurial team	All-star combination; free agents	Weak or solo entrepreneur
Industry and technical experience	Top of the field; super track record	Underdeveloped
Integrity	Highest reputation	Questionable or unknown/unrecognized
Intellectual honesty	Know what they do not know	Do not want to know what they do not know

Personal Criteria

Goals and fit	Getting what you want; but wanting what you get	Surprises, as in The Crying Game
Upside/downside issues	Attainable success/limited risks	Linear; on same continuum

(continued)

Exhibit 2.2 Venture Growth Assessment (continued)

Criteria	Highest Potential	Lowest Potential
Opportunity costs	Acceptable cuts in salary, etc.	Comfortable with status quo
Desirability	Fits with lifestyle and belief system	Simply pursuing big money
Risk/reward tolerance	Calculated risk; low risk/reward ratio	Risk averse or gambler
Stress tolerance	Thrives under pressure	Cracks under pressure
Strategic Differentiation		
Degree of fit	High	Low
Team	Best in class; excellent free agents	B team; no free agents
Service management	Superior service concept	Perceived as unimportant
Timing	Rowing with the tide	Rowing against the tide
Technology	Groundbreaking; one of a kind	Many substitutes or competitors
Flexibility	Able to adapt; commit and decommit quickly	Slow; stubborn
Opportunity orientation	Proven experience in exploiting opportunities	Operating in a vacuum; napping; hasn't made significant changes in years
Pricing	At or near leader	Undercut competitor; low prices
Distribution channels	Accessible; networks in place	Unknown; inaccessible
Room for error	Forgiving strategy	Unforgiving; rigid strategy

changed to attracting "eyeballs," which changed to page views. Many investors got caught up in "false" metrics. Those who survived the NASDAQ crash of 2000–2001 understood that dot-com survivors would be the ones who executed transactions. Numbers of customers, amounts of individual transactions, and repeat transactions became the recognized standard.[2] What are the key drivers in your industry?

Screening Criteria: The Characteristics of High-Potential Ventures

Venture capitalists, savvy entrepreneurs, and investors also use this concept of boundaries in screening ventures. Exhibit 2.1 summarizes criteria used by venture capitalists to evaluate opportunities. Their criteria tend to have a high-technology bias. As will be seen later, venture capital investors reject 60–70 percent of the new ventures presented to them very early in the review process, which focuses on how the entrepreneurs satisfy these criteria.

However, these criteria are not the exclusive domain of venture capitalists. The criteria are based on plain good business sense that is also used by successful entrepreneurs, private investors, and growth-oriented small businesses. Consider the following examples of great small companies built without a dime of professional venture capital.

- Paul Tobin, who built Cellular One in eastern Massachusetts from the ground up to $100 million in revenue in five years, started Roamer Plus with less than $300,000 of internally generated funds from other ventures. Within two years, it grew to a $15 million annual sales rate and was very profitable.
- Mark Nelson started Ovid Technologies in the late 1980s in a one-bedroom apartment in Manhattan's Spanish Harlem. Unable to find investors, he grew his company by renting more and more apartments in his building until computer network wires ran in and out of windows. Salaries for his employees were low, but at least Nelson allowed them to live rent-free in their office spaces! It was not until 1994, when Ovid had 150 employees, that he went public and raised $10 million. In 1999 he sold his company for $200 million.[3]

- In 1986 Pleasant Rowland founded the Pleasant Company mail-order catalog company as a means to distribute her line of American Girls Collection historical dolls. She had begun the company with the modest royalties she received from writing children's books and did not have enough capital to compete in stores with the likes of Mattel's Barbie.[4] By 1992 she had grown the company to $65 million in sales. Mattel acquired it in 1998 for $700 million, and under her continued management the company had sales of $300 million in 1999 and 2000.[5]

The point of departure here is opportunity and, implicitly, the customer, the marketplace, and the industry. Exhibit 2.2 shows how higher and lower potential opportunities can be placed along a desirability scale. The criteria provide some quantitative ways in which an entrepreneur can make judgments about issues concerning industry and market, competitive advantage, economics and harvesting, management team, and fatal flaw—and whether these add up to a compelling opportunity. For example, *dominant* strength in any one of these criteria can readily translate into a winning entry, whereas a flaw in a single one can be fatal.

As a small business entrepreneur, you are in a better position to decide how these criteria can be compromised. As outlined in Exhibit 2.2, businesses with the greatest potential will possess many of the following criteria, or they will dominate in one or a few for which the competition cannot come close.

Industry and Market Issues

Market. *Higher potential* businesses identify a market niche for a product or service that meets an important customer need and provides high value-added or value-created benefits to customers. Customers who are loyal to your brand or with no brand or other loyalties are reachable and receptive to the product or service (thus giving you the opportunity to seize customer loyalty). The potential payback to the user or customer of a given product or service through cost savings or other value-added or valued-created properties is one year or less and is identifiable, repeatable, and verifiable. Further, the life of the product or service exists beyond the time needed to recover the investment, plus a profit. And the company is able to expand beyond one product. If benefits to customers cannot be calculated in such dollar terms, then the market potential is far more difficult and risky to ascertain.

Lower potential opportunities are unfocused regarding customer need, and customers are unreachable and/or have brand or other loyalties to competitors. A payback to the user of more than three years and low value-added or value-created properties also makes a company unattractive. Being unable to expand beyond a one-product company can make for a lower potential opportunity. The failure of one of the first portable computer companies, Osborne Computer, is a prime example of this.

Market Structure. Market structure, such as that evidenced by the number of sellers, their size distribution, whether products are differentiated, conditions of entry and exit, number of buyers, cost conditions, and sensitivity of demand to changes in price, is significant.

A fragmented, imperfect market or emerging industry often contains vacuums and asymmetries that create unfilled market niches—for example, markets where resource ownership, cost advantages, and the like can be achieved. In addition, there are opportunities where information or knowledge gaps exist and where competition is profitable, but not so strong as to be overwhelming.

Highly concentrated and perfectly competitive industries or those that are mature or declining are typically less rewarding. The capital requirements and costs to achieve distribution and marketing presence can be prohibitive, and such behavior as price-cutting and other competitive strategies in highly concentrated markets can be a significant barrier to entry. (The most blatant example is organized crime and its life-threatening actions when territories are invaded.) Yet revenge by normal competitors, who are well positioned through product strategy, legal tactics, and the like, also can be punishing to the pocketbook.

The difficulty of operating in perfectly competitive industries is captured by this comment by prominent Boston venture capitalist William Egan: "I want to be in a nonauction market."[6]

Market Size. Companies that sell to large and growing markets (i.e., ones where capturing a small market share can represent significant and increasing sales volume) can themselves grow rapidly. A minimum market size of over $100 million in sales appears to be the threshold size to foster such growth. Such a market size means it is possible to achieve significant sales by capturing roughly 5 percent market share and thus not threatening competitors. For example, to achieve a sales level of $1 million in a $100 million market requires only 1 percent of the market. Once the small company achieves a foothold, then the foundation is in place to grow. If you are in a substantial market with 5 percent market share, then you may have an opportunity to scale into a high-value venture.

However, such a market can be too large. A multibillion-dollar market may be too mature and stable, and such a level of certainty can translate into competition from Fortune 500 firms and, if highly competitive, into lower margins and profitability. An unknown market or one that is less than $10 million in sales also presents obstacles to growth. To understand the disadvantages of a large, more mature market, consider the entry of a firm into the microcomputer industry today versus the entry of Apple Computer into that market in 1975.

Growth Rate. It is easier to capture new business from a large and growing market than it is to take business from others in a stable or declining market. An annual growth rate of 20–30 percent expands niches and indicates a market is a thriving and expansive one rather than a stable or contracting one, where competitors are scrambling for the same niches. Thus, for example, a $100 million market growing at 50 percent per year has the potential to become a $1 billion industry in a few years, affording the company with a foothold to grow substantially if it just maintains its market share over the next few years.

Market Capacity. Another signal of the existence of an opportunity in a market is a market at full capacity in a growth situation—in other words, a demand that the existing suppliers cannot meet. A growing industry where other manufacturers are at full capacity is an exciting environment. Timing is of vital concern in such a situation, which means the entrepreneur should be asking: Can I fill that demand before the other players decide to and then actually increase capacity?

Market Share Attainable. The desire and potential to be a leader in the market and capture at least a 20 percent share of the market is important and can create a very high value for a company that might otherwise be worth not much more than book value. For example, Keystone Automotive Operations, Inc., started as a supplier to hot rod builders and racers. They expanded the business in response to the explosion of SUVs in the 1990s. In 2003 the company was the nation's largest warehouse distributor of specialty parts for autos, SUVs, and light trucks.

Cost Structure. In general, firms with lower costs are more profitable; however, industries that continually face declining cost conditions place margin constraints on all participants. Interestingly, certain small firms might have great expansion potential because of low costs learned over many years. We have seen many low cost competitors that didn't realize the real value of their long experience. Where costs per unit are high when small amounts of the product are sold, existing firms that have low promotion costs can face attractive market opportunities. For instance, consider the operating leverage of Johnsonville Sausage, a manufacturing company in Wisconsin. Their variable costs were 4 percent labor and 58 percent raw materials with the remaining going to overhead, sales and marketing, and profit. What aggressive incentives could management put in place for the 4 percent to manage and to control the other costs? Imagine the disasters that would occur if the scenario were reversed!

Economics

Profits After Tax. High and durable growth margins usually translate into strong and durable after-tax profits. Opportunities that have potential for durable profits of at least 10–15 percent, and often 20 percent or more, will lure growth capital. Companies generating after-tax profits of less than 5 percent are quite fragile.

Breakeven and Positive Cash Flow. Consistent positive cash flow for a three- to five-year period indicates the economics of the company are exciting. Fluctuating between breakeven and positive cash flow, even if the degree of positive cash is significant, is a red flag.

ROI Potential. An important corollary to forgiving economics is reward. Truly high-potential opportunities have the power to yield a return on investment of 25 percent or more *per year*. After all, during the 1980s, many venture capital funds achieved only single-digit returns on investment, and since 2000 many of those same firms are in negative territory. High and durable gross margins and high and durable after-tax profits usually yield high earnings per share and high return on stockholders' equity, thus generating a satisfactory "harvest" price for a company. This is most likely true whether the company is sold through an initial public offering or is acquired. Given the risk typically involved, a return on investment potential of less than 15–20 percent per year is simply not exciting.

Capital Requirements. Capital for growth is much more accessible than capital for a new venture. The reality is that resource providers are risk averse. New ventures are speculating about markets. Small businesses with a track record have a much clearer path to success and therefore greater access to capital. Deciding who is the right capital provider for your business's growth and how to properly communicate with those providers is a subject we will tackle in depth later in the book.

Internal Rate of Return Potential. Is the risk-reward relationship attractive enough? The response to this question can be intensely personal because every individual has a different perspective on risk and return and a different personal utility curve, but the most appealing opportunities often have the promise of—and deliver on—a very substantial upside of five to ten times the original investment in five to ten years. Of course, the extraordinary successes can yield fifty to one hundred times or more, but these truly are exceptions. A 25 percent or more annual compound rate of return is considered very healthy. In 2003, those investments considered basically risk free had yields of 3–8 percent.

Free Cash Flow Characteristics.* Free cash flow is a way of understanding a number of crucial financial dimensions of any business: the robustness of its economics; its capital requirements, both working and

---

*For a more detailed description of free cash flow, see William Sahlman, "Note on Free Cash Flow Valuation Models," HBS Case 9-288-023, Harvard Business School, Rev. August 18, 2003.

fixed assets; its capacity to service external debt and equity claims; and its capacity to sustain growth. We define unleveraged free cash flow (FCF) as

Earnings before interest but after taxes (EBIAT)

Plus   Amortization (A) and depreciation (D)

Less   Spontaneous working capital requirements (WC)

Less   Capital expenditures (CAPex),

or

FCF = EBIAT + [A+D] − [+ or −WC] − CAPex.

EBIAT is driven by sales, profitability, and asset intensity. Low-asset-intensive, high-margin businesses generate the highest profits and sustainable growth.[7]

Gross Margins. High and durable gross margins (i.e., the unit selling price less all direct and variable costs), or at least the potential to achieve them with growth, is important. Gross margins exceeding 40–50 percent provide a tremendous built-in cushion that allows for more error and more flexibility to learn from mistakes than do gross margins of 20 percent or less. High and durable gross margins, in turn, mean that a venture can reach breakeven earlier, an event that preferably occurs within the first two years. Thus, for example, if gross margins are just 20 percent, for every $1 increase in fixed costs (e.g., insurance, salaries, rent, and utilities), sales need to increase $5 just to stay even. If gross margins are 75 percent, however, a $1 increase in fixed costs requires a sales increase of just $1.33. R. Douglas Kahn, an entrepreneur who built the international division of an emerging software company to $17 million in highly profitable sales in just five years (when he was twenty-five years of age), offers an example of the cushion provided by high and durable gross margins. He stresses there is simply no substitute for outrageous gross margins: "It allows you to make all kinds of mistakes that would kill a normal company. And we made them all. But our high gross margins covered all the learning tuition and still left a good profit."[8] Gross margins of less than 20 percent, particularly when they are fragile, are a red flag.

Harvest Issues

Value-Added Potential. Companies that have strategic value in an industry, such as important technology, are intrinsically more valuable than those with low or no strategic value. Opportunities with extremely large capital commitments, whose value on exit can be severely eroded by unanticipated circumstances, are less interesting to the capital markets. Nuclear power is a good example. Niche dot-coms proved to be another.

Thus, one characteristic of businesses that command a premium price is that they have high value-added strategic importance to their acquirer: distribution, customer base, geographic coverage, proprietary technology, contractual rights, and the like. Such companies might be valued at four, five, or even six times (or more) last year's *sales*, whereas perhaps 60–80 percent of companies might be purchased at .75 to .04 times sales.

Valuation Multiples and Comparables. Consistent with the previous point, there is a large spread in the value the capital markets place on private and public companies. Part of your analysis is to identify some of the historical boundaries for valuations placed on companies in the market/industry/technology area in which you compete. The rules of thumb outlined in Exhibit 2.1 are variable and should be thought of as a boundary and a point of departure.

Exit Mechanism and Strategy. Businesses that are eventually sold—privately or to the public—usually are started and grown with a harvest objective in mind. Planning is critical because, as is often said, it is much harder to get out of a business than to get into it. Giving some serious thought to the options and likelihood that the company can eventually be harvested is an important initial and ongoing aspect of the entrepreneurial process.

Capital Market Context. The context in which the sale or acquisition of the company takes place is largely driven by the capital market context at that particular point in time. Timing can be a critical component of the exit mechanism because, as one study indicated, since World War II the average bull market on Wall Street has lasted just six months. For a keener appreciation of the critical difference the capital markets can make, recall the stock market crash of October 19, 1987, the prolonged bear market of 2000–2003, or the bank credit crunch of 1990–1992. Initial public offerings are especially vulnerable to the fluctuations of the capital markets; here the timing is vital. Some of the most successful companies grow when debt and equity capital were most available and relatively cheap.

Competitive Advantages Issues

Variable and Fixed Costs. An attractive opportunity has the potential for being the lowest-cost producer and for having the lowest costs of marketing and distribution. For example, Bowmar was unable to remain competitive in the market for electronic calculators after the producers of large-scale integrated circuits, such as Hewlett-Packard, entered the business. Being unable to achieve and sustain a position as a low-cost producer shortens the life expectancy of a new venture.

Degree of Control. Desirable opportunities have potential for moderate-to-strong degree of control over prices, costs, and channels of distribution. Fragmented markets where there is no dominant competitor—no Microsoft operating system—have this potential. These markets usually have a market leader with a 20 percent market share *or less*. For example, sole control of the source of supply of a critical component for a product or of channels of distribution can give a new venture market dominance even if other areas are weak. Lack of control over such factors as product development and component prices constrain an opportunity. A market where a major competitor has a market share of 40 percent, 50 percent, or especially 60 percent usually implies one in which power and influence over suppliers, customers, and pricing create a serious barrier and risk for a new firm. Such a firm will have few degrees of freedom. However, if a dominant competitor is at full capacity, is slow to innovate or to add capacity in a large and growing market, or routinely ignores or abuses the customer (remember "Ma Bell"), there may be an entry opportunity. However, entrepreneurs usually do not find such sleepy competition in dynamic, emerging industries dense with opportunity.

Entry Barriers. Having a favorable window of opportunity is important. Having or being able to gain proprietary protection, regulatory advantage, or other legal or contractual advantage, such as exclusive rights to a market or with a distributor, is important to a durable opportunity. Having or being able to gain an advantage in response/lead times is important, since these can create barriers to entry or expansion by others. For example, advantages in response/lead times in technology, product innovation, market innovation, people, location, resources, or capacity enhance the potential of an opportunity. Possession of well-developed, high-quality, accessible contacts that are the product of years of building a top-notch reputation and that cannot be acquired quickly is also advantageous. In fact, there are times when this competitive advantage may be so strong as to provide dominance in the marketplace, even though many of the other factors are weak or average. An example of how quickly the joys of entrepreneurship may fade if others cannot be kept out is the experience of firms in the hard-disk industry that were unable to erect entry barriers in the United States in the early to mid-1980s. By the end of 1983, some ninety hard-drive companies were launched, and severe price competition led to a major industry shakeout. Take a look at the cell-phone business. During the 2003 Christmas holidays there were seventeen different cell-phone retailers on Oxford Street in London in a linear mile! If a firm cannot keep others out or if it faces already existing entry barriers, it can get lost in a fragmented market. An easily overlooked issue is a firm's capacity to gain distribution of its product. As simple as it may sound, even venture-capital-backed companies fall victim to this market issue. Air Florida apparently assembled all the right ingredients, including substantial financing, yet was unable to secure sufficient gate space for its airplanes. Even though it sold passenger seats, it had no place to pick the passengers up or drop them off.

Management Team Issues

Entrepreneurial Team. The best opportunities have existing teams that are strong and contain industry superstars. The team has proven profit-and-loss experience in the same technology, market, and service area, and members have complementary and compatible skills.

Industry and Technical Experience. A management track record of significant accomplishment in the industry, proven profit using technology in the market area, and lots of achievements where the venture will compete is highly desirable. A top-notch management team can become the most important strategic competitive advantage in an industry. Imagine relocating the Chicago Bulls or the Phoenix Suns to Halifax, Nova Scotia: do you think you would have a winning competitor in the National Basketball Association?

Integrity. Trust and integrity are the oil and glue that make economic interdependence possible. Having an unquestioned reputation in this regard is a major long-term advantage for entrepreneurs and should be sought in all personnel and backers. A shady past is for B team players only.

Intellectual Honesty. There is a fundamental issue of whether the founders recognize what they do and do not know, as well as whether they know what to do about shortcomings or gaps in the team and the enterprise.

Fatal-Flaw Issues. Basically, ventures cannot have fatal flaws; an opportunity is terminal if it suffers from one or more fatal flaws. Usually, these relate to one of the above criteria, and examples abound of markets that are too small, that have overpowering competition, where the cost of entry is too high, where an entrant is unable to produce at a competitive price, and so on. Air Florida provides another example here: a second fatal flaw was the company's inability to get flights listed on reservation computers.

Personal Criteria

Goals and Fit. Is there a good match between the requirements of business and what the founders want out of it? A very wise woman, Dorothy Stevenson, pinpointed the crux of it with this powerful insight: "Success is getting what you want. Happiness is wanting what you get."

Upside/Downside Issues. Informed investors always examine an opportunity's downside risk. The upside and the downside of pursuing an opportunity are not linear, nor are they on the same continuum. The upside is easy, and it has been said that success has a thousand sires. The downside is quite another matter, since it has also been said that failure is an orphan. An entrepreneur needs to be able to absorb the financial downside in such a way that he or she can rebound, without becoming indentured to debt obligations. If an entrepreneur's financial exposure in launching the venture is greater than his or her net worth—the resources he or she can reasonably draw upon, and his or her alternative disposable earnings stream if it does not work out—the deal may be too big. While today's bankruptcy laws are generous, the psychological burdens of living through such an ordeal are infinitely more painful than the financial consequences. In addition to fiscal matters, an existing business needs to consider whether a failure will be too demeaning to the firm's reputation and future credibility.[9]

Opportunity Cost. In pursuing any venture opportunity, there are also opportunity costs. An entrepreneur who is skilled enough to grow a successful, multimillion-dollar venture has talents that are highly valued by medium- to large-sized firms as well. While assessing benefits that may accrue in pursuing an opportunity, an entrepreneur needs to take a serious look at other alternatives, including potential "golden handcuffs," and account honestly for any cut in salary that may be involved in pursuing a certain opportunity.

Further, pursuing an opportunity can shape an entrepreneur in ways that are hard to imagine. An entrepreneur will probably have time to execute between two to four multimillion-dollar ventures between the ages of twenty-five and fifty. Each of these experiences will position her or him, *for better or for worse*, for the next opportunity.

Desirability. A good opportunity is desirable to (i.e., the good opportunity fits) the entrepreneur and investors. An intensely personal criterion would be the desire for a certain lifestyle. This may preclude pursuing certain opportunities (i.e., those may become opportunities for someone else). The founder of a major high-technology venture in the Boston area was asked why the headquarters of his firm was located in downtown Boston, while those of other such firms were located on the famous Route 128 outside of the city. His reply was that he wanted to live in Boston because he loved the city and wanted to be able to walk to work. He said, "The rest did not matter."

Risk/Reward Tolerance. Successful entrepreneurs take calculated risks or avoid risks they do not need to take; as a country-and-western song puts it: "You have to know when to hold 'em, know when to fold 'em, know when to walk away, and know when to run." This is not to suggest that all entrepreneurs are gamblers or have the same risk tolerance; some are quite conservative while others actually seem to get a kick out of the inherent danger and thrill in higher risk and higher stake games. The real issue is fit—recognizing that gamblers and overly risk-averse entrepreneurs are unlikely to sustain any long-term successes.

Stress Tolerance. Another important dimension of the fit concept is the stressful requirements of a fast-growth, high-stakes venture. Or as President Harry Truman said so well: "If you can't stand the heat, then stay out of the kitchen."

Strategic Differentiation

Degree of Fit. To what extent is there a good fit among the driving forces (founders and team, opportunity, and resource requirements) and the timing given the external environment?

Team. There is no substitute for an absolute top quality team, since the execution and the ability to adapt and to devise constantly new strategies is so vital to survival and success. A team is nearly unstoppable if it can inculcate into the venture a philosophy and culture of superior learning, as well as teaching skills, an ethic of high standards, delivery of results, and constant improvement. Are they free agents—clear of employment, noncompete, proprietary-rights, and trade-secret agreements—who are able to pursue the opportunity?

Service Management. Several years back the Forum Corporation of Boston conducted research across a wide range of industries with several hundred companies to determine why customers stopped buying these companies' products. The results were surprising: 15 percent of the customers defected because of quality and 70 percent stopped using a product or service because of bad customer service. Having a "turbo-service" concept that can be delivered consistently can be a major competitive weapon against small and large competitors alike. Home Depot, in the home supply business, and Lexus, in the auto industry, have set an entirely new standard of service for their respective industries.

Timing. From business to historic military battles to political campaigns, timing is often the one element that can make a significant difference. Time can be an enemy or a friend; being too early or too late can be fatal. The key is to row with the tide, not against it. Strategically, ignoring this principle is perilous.

Technology. A breakthrough, proprietary product is no guarantee of success, but it certainly creates a formidable competitive advantage (see Exhibit 2.3).

Flexibility. Maintaining the capacity to commit and decommit quickly, to adapt, and to abandon if necessary is a major strategic weapon, particularly when competing with larger organizations. Larger firms can typically take six years or more to change basic strategy and ten to twenty years or more to change the culture.

Opportunity Orientation. To what extent is there a constant alertness to the marketplace? A continual search for opportunities? As one insightful entrepreneur put it, "Any opportunity that just comes in the door to us, we do not consider an opportunity. And we do not have a strategy until we are saying no to lots of opportunities."

Pricing. One of the most common mistakes of new companies, with high value-added products or services in a growing market, is to underprice. A price slightly below to as much as 20 percent below competi-

Exhibit 2.3 Major Inventions by U.S. Small Firms in the 20th Century

Acoustical suspension speakers	Heterodyne radio
Aerosol cans	High-capacity computer
Air-conditioning	Hydraulic brake
Airplane	Learning machine
Artificial skin	Link trainer
Assembly line	Nuclear magnetic resonance
Automatic fabric cutting	Plezo electronic devices
Automatic transfer equipment	Polaroid camera
Bakelite	Prefabricated housing
Biosynthetic insulin	Pressure-sensitive cellophane
Catalytic petroleum cracking	Quick-frozen foods
Continuous casting	Rotary oil drilling bit
Cotton picker	Safety razor
Fluid flow meter	Six-axis robot arm
Fosin fire extinguisher	Soft contact lenses
Geodesic dome	Sonar fish monitoring
Heart valve	Spectographic grid
Heat sensor	Stereographic image sensoring
Helicopter	

Source: Small Business Association

tors is rationalized as necessary to gain market entry. In a 30 percent gross margin business, a 10 percent price increase results in a 20–36 percent increase in gross margin and will lower the break-even sales level of a company with $900,000 in fixed costs to $2.5 million from $3 million. At the $3 million sales level, the company would realize an extra $180,000 in pretax profits.

Distribution Channels. Having access to the distribution channels is sometimes overlooked or taken for granted. New channels of distribution can leapfrog and demolish traditional channels; take for instance, direct mail, home shopping networks, infomercials, and the coming revolution in interactive television in your own home.

Room for Error. How forgiving is the business and the financial strategy? How wrong can the team be in estimates of revenue costs, cash flow, timing, and capital requirements? How bad can things get, yet be able to survive? If some single engine planes are more prone to accidents, by ten times or more, which plane do you want to fly in? High leverage, lower gross margins, and lower operating margins are the signals in a small company of these flights destined for fatality.

Conclusion

Complacency is the first symptom of a terminally ill company. Usually, that rut is formed because a small firm either becomes comfortable with a seemingly consistent revenue stream or is spending all its time fighting day-to-day fires. The result is a detachment from market dynamics and lost vision about why the company was originally founded. Successful entrepreneurs are personally and organizationally self-reflective. Staying close to your entrepreneurial roots means constantly reassessing the nature of the opportunity and your firm's ability to exploit market needs. That knowledge affords you the power to be strategic in your plans to grow and then reap large capital gains. We hope this chapter has motivated you to do the hard work of reflection and assessment that will provide the foundation of knowledge required to grow your company.

Notes

1. See J. A. Timmons, D. F. Muzyka, H. H. Stevenson, and W. D. Bygrave, "Opportunity Recognition: The Core of Entrepreneurship," in *Frontiers of Entrepreneurship Research*, ed. Neil Churchill et al. (Babson Park, MA: Babson College, 1987), p. 409.

2. Ernie Parizeau, partner, Norwest Ventures, in a speech to Babson College MBAs, Dec. 2000.

3. Sarah Schafer, "Start-Up Sizzled Without Venture Capital," *Washington Post*, June 27, 1999, p. H7.

4. Mollie Neal, "Cataloger Gets Pleasant Results," *Direct Marketing*, May 1992, p. 33.

5. Brian Dumaine, "How to Compete with a Champ," *Fortune*, Jan. 10, 1994, p. 106.

6. Comment made during a presentation at Babson College, May 1985.

7. William A. Sahlman, "Sustainable Growth Analysis," HBS 9-284-059, Harvard Business School, 1984.

8. R. Douglas Kahn, president, Interactive Images, Inc., speaking in 1991 in Jeffry Timmons's class at Babson College about his experiences as international marketing director at McCormack & Dodge from 1978 through 1983.

9. This point was made by J. Willard Marriott Jr. at Founder's Day at Babson College, 1988.

CHAPTER 3

TEAM BUILDING

"The way a team plays as a whole determines its success. You may have the greatest bunch of individual stars in the world, but if they don't play together, the club won't be worth a dime."

—BABE RUTH

The Entrepreneurial Approach to Resources

Resources include (1) people, such as the management team, the board of directors, lawyers, accountants, and consultants; (2) financial resources; (3) assets, such as plant and equipment; and (4) your existing business, but especially the customer base and industry network understanding. Successful entrepreneurs view the need for and the ownership and management of these resources in the pursuit of opportunities differently from the way managers in many large organizations view them. Remember, great entrepreneurs create or seize an opportunity and pursue it *regardless of the resources currently controlled.**

*This definition was developed by Howard H. Stevenson and colleagues at the Harvard Business School. His work on a paradigm for entrepreneurial management has contributed greatly to this area of entrepreneurship. See Howard H. Stevenson, "A New Paradigm for Entrepreneurial Management," in *Proceedings from the 7th Anniversary Symposium on Entrepreneurship*, July 1983 (Boston: Harvard Business School, 1984).

Deciding what resources are needed, when they are needed, and how to acquire them are strategies that fit with the other driving forces of entrepreneurship. Your role as a leader of an organization is to use the minimum possible amount of all types of resources at each stage in your venture's growth. Rather than own the resources, seek to control them.

Consider some basic approaches to pursue growth with reduced risk:

Staged Capital Commitments

"Staging" capital means using only the resources necessary to get you to a higher level of value in your business. The capital infusions are staged to match critical milestones that will signal whether it is prudent to keep going, and thus infuse the second stage of capital, or abort the effort at growth. Both the founder's and investor's financial exposure, and dilution of equity ownership, is reduced.

- **Capital.** The amount of capital required is simply smaller, thereby reducing the financial exposure and the dilution of the founder's equity.
- **Flexibility.** Entrepreneurs who do not own a resource are in a better position to commit and decommit quickly.[1] One price of ownership of resources is an inherent inflexibility. With the rapidly fluctuating conditions and uncertainty with which most entrepreneurial ventures have to contend, inflexibility can be a serious curse. Response times need to be short if a firm is to be competitive. Most time-decision windows are small and elusive. And while it can be difficult to predict accurately the resources that will be necessary to grow, you have an industry knowledge advantage. In addition to being nimble, the entrepreneurial approach to resources permits iterations or strategic experiments in the venture process—that is, ideas can be tried and tested without committing to the ownership of all assets and resources in the business, to markets and technology that change rapidly, and so forth. Consider also, for example, the inflexibility of a company that commits permanently to a certain technology, software, or management system.

- **Low sunk cost.** Sunk costs are lower if the firm exercises the option to abort a plan at any point. Consider, instead, the enormous up-front capital commitment of a nuclear power plant and the cost of abandoning such a project.
- **Costs.** Fixed costs are lowered, thus favorably affecting breakeven. Of course, the other side of the coin is that variable costs may rise. But if your business model doesn't provide forgiving and rewarding economics, you shouldn't be growing! If it is, then there still will most likely be ample gross margins in the venture to absorb this rise.
- **Reduced risk.** In addition to reducing total exposure, other risks, such as the risk of obsolescence of the resource, are also lower.

It is a myth that a company that cannot afford a resource shouldn't be growing. The truth is that not owning resources provides advantages and options. Of course, these decisions are extremely complex, involving such details as the tax implications of leasing versus buying and so forth.

Bootstrapping Strategies: Marshaling and Minimizing Resources

Minimizing resources is referred to in colloquial terms as bootstrapping, or, more formally, as a lack of resource intensity, defined as a multistage commitment of resources with a minimum commitment at each stage or decision point.[2] When discussing his philosophy on bootstrapping, Greg Gianforte (who retired at the age of thirty-three after he and his partners sold their software business, Brightwork Development Inc., to McAfee Associates) stated "a lot of entrepreneurs think they need money . . . when actually they haven't figured out the business equation."[3] According to Gianforte, lack of money, employees, equipment—even lack of product—is actually a huge advantage, because it forces the boot-strapper to concentrate on selling to bring cash into the business. Thus, to persevere, entrepreneurs ask at every step how they can accomplish a little more with a little less and pursue growth.

As was outlined in Exhibit 1.2, just the opposite attitude is often evident in large institutions that usually are characterized by a trustee or custodial viewpoint. Managers in larger institutions seek to have not only enough committed resources for the task at hand but also a cushion against the tough times.

Build Your Brain Trust

Team building begins with an honest assessment of the current players in your company. Evaluating the team must be done in the context of the growth plan you are pursuing. That plan dictates the skills necessary to achieve your goals. Take, for example, Eric Johnson. Eric purchased Baldwin Ice Cream Co. in 1997 when it had total sales of under $2 million. Then, he purchased Richardson Foods in 1999. The combined sales of the company were under $6 million. "I had a plan to grow. And you don't grow a company without an 'A' team. Together we established aggressive goals for the company and for the leadership. People that couldn't or wouldn't keep up usually opted out. We recruited some new players, forming a truly 'A' team." Baldwin Richardson Foods will top $70 million in sales in 2003. Eric Johnson knew what he needed to fill in the gaps on the team. He focused on identifying individuals with the know-how, experience, and networks that have access to critical talent, experience, and resources that can make the difference between success and failure.

Using Other People's Resources (OPR)

Obtaining the use of other people's resources, particularly in the start-up and early growth stages of a venture, is an important approach for entrepreneurs. In contrast, large firms assume that virtually all resources have to be owned to control their use, and decisions center around how these resources will be acquired and financed—not so with entrepreneurs.

The key is having the use of the resource and being able to control or influence the deployment of the resource. Other people's resources can include, for example, money invested or loaned by friends, relatives, business associates, or other investors. Or resources can include people, space, equipment, or other material loaned, provided inexpensively or free by customers or suppliers, or secured by bartering future services. In fact, using other people's resources can be as simple as benefiting from free booklets and pamphlets, such as those published by many of the Big Four accounting firms, or making use of low-cost educational programs or of government-funded management assistance programs.

How can you begin to tap into these resources? Howard H. Stevenson and William H. Sahlman suggest that you do "two seemingly contradictory things: seek out the best advisors—specialists if you have to—and involve them more thoroughly, and at an earlier stage, than you have in the past. At the same time, be more skeptical of their credentials and their advice."[4] A recent study found that social capital, including having an established business network and encouragement from friends and family, is strongly associated with entrepreneurial activity.[5]

Exhibit 3.1 Hypotheses Concerning Networks and Entrepreneurial Effectiveness

Effective entrepreneurs are more likely than others to systematically plan and monitor network activities.
- Effective entrepreneurs are able to *chart their present network* and to discriminate between productive and symbolic ties.
- Effective entrepreneurs are able to *view effective networks as a crucial aspect for ensuring the success of their company.*
- Effective entrepreneurs are able to *stabilize and maintain networks,* in order to increase their effectiveness and their efficiency.

Effective entrepreneurs are more likely than others to undertake actions toward increasing their network density and diversity.
- Effective entrepreneurs set aside time for purely random activities—things done with no specific problem in mind.
- Effective entrepreneurs are able to *check network density,* to avoid too many overlaps (because they affect network efficiency) while still attaining solidarity and cohesiveness.
- Effective entrepreneurs multiply, through extending the reachability of their networks, the stimuli for better and faster adaptation to change.

We would add:
- Effective entrepreneurs are able to *leverage and create value for their networks.*

Source: Adapted from Paola Dubini and Howard Aldrich, "Executive Forum: Personal and Extended Networks Are Central to the Entrepreneurial Process," *Journal of Business Venturing* 6, no. 5. (September 1991): pp. 310–12. Reprinted with permission from Elsevier.

In addition to networking with family, friends, classmates, and advisors, Stevenson and Sahlman suggest that the human touch enhances the relationship between the entrepreneur and the advisors to the venture.[6] Accuracy in social perception, skill at impression management, skill at persuasion and influence, and a high level of social adaptability may be relevant to the activities necessary for successful new ventures.[7]

There are many examples of controlling people resources, rather than owning them. In real estate, even the largest firms do not employ top architects full-time but rather secure them on a project basis. Most smaller firms do not employ lawyers but obtain legal assistance as needed. Technical consultants, design engineers, and programmers are other examples.

Outside People Resources

Board of Directors

Deciding whether to have a board of directors and, if the answer is yes, choosing and finding the people who will sit on the board, can be troublesome for new ventures.*

The Decision. If your firm is organized as a corporation, it *must* have a board of directors, elected by the shareholders. There is flexibility with other forms of organization. However, many small firms do not have a board, and many who do fill it with friends and insiders. Our message is that the board should comprise people who are linked to key aspects of the opportunity you seek to grow. In addition, certain investors will require a board of directors. Venture capitalists almost always require boards of directors—and that they be represented on the boards. Beyond that, deciding to involve outsiders is worth careful thought. This decision starts with the identification of missing relevant experience, know-how, and networks, and of what the venture needs at this stage of its development that can be provided by outside directors.

*The authors are indebted to Howard H. Stevenson of the Harvard Business School and to Leslie Charm and Karl Youngman of Doktor Pet Centers and Command Performance hair salons, respectively, for sharing their insights concerning boards of directors.

Their probable contributions then can be balanced against the fact that having a board of directors will necessitate greater disclosure of plans for operating and financing the business. It also is worth noting that one of the responsibilities of a board of directors is to elect officers for the firm, affecting decisions about financing and the ownership of the voting shares in the company.

It can be argued that the makeup of the boards of the Internet IPOs that flooded the market between 1998 and 2000 might have been flawed because they were dominated by company executives and venture capitalists. Some argue that at least half of the board members be outside directors.[8]

When Art Spinner of Hambro International was interviewed by *Inc.*, he explained that entrepreneurs worry about the wrong thing ". . . that the boards are going to steal their companies or take them over." Though entrepreneurs have many reasons to worry, that's not one of them. It almost never happens. In truth, boards don't even have much power. They are less well equipped to police entrepreneurs than to advise them.[9]

As Spinner suggests, the expertise that members of a board can bring to a venture, at a price it can afford, can far outweigh any of the negative factors. David Gumpert and his partner in what was originally Net-Marquee (an online direct marketing agency) chose their advisory board by focusing on "holes" that needed to be filled, while also being mindful of financial constraints. According to Gumpert, "the board continually challenged us—in terms of tactics, strategy, and overall business philosophy." These challenges benefited their company in three ways: (1) prevented dumb mistakes, (2) kept them focused on what really mattered, and (3) kept them from getting gloomy.[10]

Selection Criteria: Add Value with Know-How and Contacts. Finding the appropriate people for the board is a challenge. It is important to be objective and to select individuals who are known to be trustworthy. For their first outside directors, most ventures typically look to personal acquaintances of the lead entrepreneur or the team or to their lawyers, bankers, accountants, or consultants. While such a choice might be the right one for a venture, the process also involves finding the right people to fill the gaps discovered in the process of forming the management team. This issue of filling in the gaps relates back to one of the criteria of a successful management team: intellectual honesty—that is, realizing what you know and what you need to know. In a study of boards and specifically venture capitalists' contribution to them, entrepreneurs seemed to value operating experience over financial expertise.[11] In addition, the study reported that "those CEOs with a top-20 venture capital firm as the lead investor, on average did rate the value of the advice from their venture capital board members significantly higher—but not outstandingly higher—than the advice from other outside board members."[12] Defining expectations and minimum requirements for board members might be a good way to get the most out of a board of directors.

A top-notch outside director usually spends *at least* nine to ten days per year on his or her responsibilities. Four days per year are spent for quarterly meetings, a day of preparation for each meeting, a day for another meeting to cope with an unanticipated issue, plus up to a day or more for various phone calls. Yearly fees are usually paid for such a commitment. Quality directors become involved for the learning and professional development opportunities, and so forth, rather than for the money. Compensation to board members varies widely. Fees can range from as little as $500–$1,000 for a half- or full-day meeting to $30,000 per year for four to six full-day to day-and-a-half meetings, plus accessibility on a continual basis. Directors are also usually reimbursed for expenses incurred in preparing for and attending meetings. Stock in a start-up company (often 2–5 percent) or options (for 5,000–50,000 shares) are common incentives to attract and reward directors. Additionally, Art Spinner, a director of eleven companies and an advisor to two others, suggested the following as a simple set of rules to guide you toward a productive relationship with your board:[13]

- Treat your directors as individual resources.
- Always be honest with your directors.
- Set up a compensation committee.
- Set up an audit committee.
- *Never* set up an executive committee.

People who could be potential board members are increasingly cautious about getting involved, for several reasons:

- **Sarbanes-Oxley legislation.*** The Sarbanes-Oxley Act of 2002 is the most sweeping legislation affecting corporate governance, disclosure, and financial accounting in more than a generation. Sections 302 and 404 require that CEOs, CFOs, and independent auditors and committees
  — Certify the accuracy of financial statements and disclosures
  — Indicate in each periodic report whether or not there were significant changes in internal controls or related factors since their most recent evaluation, and disclose all deficiencies in the design or operation of internal controls
  — Provide an auditor's attestation to, and report on, management's assessment of the internal controls and procedures for financial reporting
  — Report that controls and procedures for financial reporting and disclosure have been evaluated for effectiveness within the past ninety days

  Specifically, Section 404 requires an annual evaluation of internal controls and procedures for financial reporting. Under this scheme, a corporation must document its existing controls that have a bearing on financial reporting, test them for efficacy, and report on gaps and deficiencies. Furthermore, the company's independent auditor must issue a report, to be included in the company's annual report, that attests to management's assertion on the effectiveness of internal controls and procedures and financial reporting.

- **Liability.** Directors of a company can be held personally liable for its actions and those of its officers, and, worse, a climate of litigation exists in many areas. For example, some specific grounds for liability of a director have included voting a dividend that renders the corporation insolvent, voting to authorize a loan out of corporate assets

*See openpages.com/solutions/openbooks/404.asp for a detailed perspective on Sarbanes-Oxley.

to a director or an officer who ultimately defaults, and signing a false corporate document or report. Courts have held that if a director acts in good faith, he or she can be excused from liability. The challenge, however, is *proving* that a director has acted in good faith. Such proof is complicated by several factors, including possibly an inexperienced management team, the financial weaknesses and cash crises that occur and demand solution, and the lack of good and complete information and records, which are necessary as the basis for action. In recent years, many states have passed what is known as the "dumb director law." In effect, the law allows that directors are normal human beings who can make mistakes and misjudgments; it goes a long way in taking the sting out of potential lawsuits that are urged by ambulance chasers.

- **Harassment.** Outside stockholders, who may have acquired stock through a private placement or through the over-the-counter market, can have unrealistic expectations about the risk involved in the venture and the speed at which a return can be realized, as well as the size of the return. Such stockholders are a source of continual annoyance for boards and for their companies.

- **Time and risk.** Experienced directors know that often it takes more time and intense involvement to work with a venture with sales of $10 million or less than with one having sales of $25 million to $50 million or more, and the former is riskier. One solution to liability concerns is for the firm to purchase indemnity insurance for its directors. But this insurance is expensive. Despite the liability problems noted above, the survey mentioned found that just 11 percent of the respondents reported difficulty in recruiting board members.[14] In dealing with this issue, new ventures will want to examine a possible director's attitude toward risk in general and evaluate whether this is the type of attitude the team needs to have represented.

Alternatives to a Formal Board. Advisors and quasi boards can be a useful alternative to having a formal board of directors.[15] A board of advisors is designed to dispense advice rather than make decisions, and therefore advisors are not exposed to personal liability. A firm can solicit objective observations and feedback from these advisors. Such informal boards can contribute needed expertise, without the legal entanglements and formalities of a regular board. Also, the possible embarrassment of having to remove someone who is not serving a useful role can be avoided. Informal advisors are usually much less expensive, with common honorariums of $500 to $1,000 per meeting. However, the level of involvement of these advisors probably will be less than members of a formal board. The firm also does not enjoy the protection of law, which defines the obligations and responsibilities of board members of a formal board.

But an informal group of advisors can be a good mechanism through which a new venture can observe a number of people in action and select one or two as regular directors. The entrepreneur gains the advantages of counsel and advice from outsiders without being legally bound by their decisions.

Attorneys

The Decision. Almost all companies need and use the services of attorneys, entrepreneurial ventures perhaps more so.* By following some legal basics and acquiring appropriate legal services, companies can achieve better legal health, including fewer problems and lower costs over the long term.[16] According to FindLaw, Inc., the factors to consider in choosing an attorney include availability, comfort level with the attorney, experience level and appropriateness to case, cost, and whether the lawyer knows the industry and has connections to investors and venture capital.[17]

Just how attorneys are used by growth-oriented ventures depends on the needs of the venture at its particular stage. Size is a factor. Exhibit 3.2 summarizes the findings of a survey by *Inc.* magazine. The trend has been for firms with sales under $1 million to use attorneys mostly for contracts

*The authors wish to acknowledge the input provided by Gerald Feigen of the Center for Entrepreneurial Studies, University of Maryland, from a course on entrepreneurship and the law he has developed and teaches at George Washington University Law School; also John Van Slyke of Alta Research.

Exhibit 3.2 How Attorneys Are Used

Annual Company Sales (% of respondents)	Less than $1 Million	$1–$2.9 Million	$3–$4.9 Million	$5–$24.9 Million	$25 Million
Legal Service Used (ranked by total mentions)					
Contracts and agreements	70%	74%	69%	84%	85%
Personal needs of top management	46	58	56	53	38
Formal litigation	34	50	63	61	91
Real estate and insurance matters	32	35	50	51	56
Incorporation	45	34	39	33	24
Estate planning	23	42	48	44	17
Delinquent accounts	20	33	39	34	21
Liability protection	20	17	22	33	41
Copyrights, trademarks, and patents	21	19	24	28	38
Mergers and acquisitions	12	14	29	32	47
Employee benefit plans	10	26	19	27	27
Tax planning and review	13	17	22	17	12
Employee stock ownership plans	9	15	10	18	21
Franchising and licensing	13	11	14	14	12
Government-required reports	8	6	6	10	12
Prospectus for public offering	2	1	5	2	18
Labor relations	1	2	2	3	3

and agreements. These companies also use a substantial amount of their attorneys' time for the personal needs of top management, matters surrounding incorporation, and formal litigation.

The necessity of legal counsel is obvious when it comes to contracts and lawsuits. But small business managers also rely on company attorneys for personal problems ranging from tax matters to divorce and estate probate. As company size increases, so does the need for advice in such areas as liability, mergers, and benefit plans.

- **Contracts and agreements.** Firms need assistance with contracts, licenses, leases, and agreements governing noncompete employment and the vesting rights of shareholders.
- **Formal litigation, liability protection, and so on.** In today's litigious climate, sooner or later most entrepreneurs will find themselves as defendants in lawsuits and require counsel.
- **Real estate, insurance, and other matters.** It is hard to imagine an entrepreneur who, at one time or another, will not be involved in various kinds of real estate transactions, from rentals to the purchase and sale of property, that require the services of an attorney.
- **Copyrights, trademarks, patents, and intellectual property protection.** Products are hard to protect. But pushing ahead with their development (software, for example) before ample protection from the law is provided can be expedient in the short term but disastrous in the long term.
- **Employee plans.** Benefit and stock ownership plans can be powerful incentives in building a team, but they have become complicated to use effectively and to administer. They require the special knowhow of lawyers so common pitfalls can be avoided.
- **Tax planning and review.** Here, a word of caution is in order. All too frequently the tail of the accountant's tax avoidance advice wags the dog of good business sense. Entrepreneurs who worry more about finding good opportunities to make money, rather than tax shelters, are infinitely better off.
- **Federal, state, and other regulations and reports.** Understanding the impact of and complying with regulations often is not easy. Violations of federal, state, and other regulations often can have serious consequences.

- **Mergers and acquisitions.** There is specialized legal know-how in buying or selling a company. Unless an entrepreneur is highly experienced and has highly qualified legal advisors in these transactions, he or she can either lose the deal or end up having to live with legal obligations that may be costly. This is especially important for the growing firm.
- **Bankruptcy law.** Many people have heard tales of entrepreneurs who did not make deposits to pay various federal and state taxes in order to use that cash in their business. It is likely that these entrepreneurs falsely assumed that if their companies went bankrupt, the government was out of luck, just like the banks and other creditors. They were wrong. In fact the owners, officers, and often the directors are held personally liable for those obligations.
- **Other matters.** These matters can range from assistance with collecting delinquent accounts to labor relations.
- **Personal needs.** As entrepreneurs accumulate net worth (i.e., property and other assets), legal advice in estate, tax, and financial planning is important.

Bankers and Other Lenders

The Decision. Deciding whether to have a banker or another lender usually involves decisions about how to finance certain needs. It appears that most companies will need the services of a banker or other lender at some time in this respect. The decision also can involve how a banker or other lender can serve as an advisor.

As with other advisors, the banker or other lender needs to be a partner, not a difficult minority shareholder. First and foremost, therefore, an entrepreneur will be well advised to select the right *banker or lender* rather than focusing only on a bank or a financial institution. Different bankers and lenders, and the institutions with whom they are affiliated, have reputations ranging from "excellent" to "just OK" to "not OK" in how they work with entrepreneurial companies. Ideally, an entrepreneur will work with an excellent banker or lender with an excellent financial institution, although an excellent banker or lender with a just-OK institution is preferable to a just-OK banker or lender with an excellent institution.

An important starting point for the entrepreneur is identifying what he or she needs from a lender. Some will have needs that are asset based, such as money for equipment, facilities, or inventory. Others may require working capital to fund short-term operating expenses.

Having a business plan is invaluable preparation for selecting and working with a lender. Also, since a banker or other lender is a "partner," it is important to invite him or her to see the company in operation, to avoid late financial statements (as well as late payments and overdrafts), and to always be honest and straightforward in sharing information.

Accountants

The Decision. The accounting profession has come a long way from the "green eyeshades" stereotype one hears reference to occasionally. Today, virtually all of the larger accounting firms have discovered the enormous client potential of new and entrepreneurial ventures, and a significant part of their business strategy is to cater specifically to these firms. In the Boston area, for instance, the leading Big Four accounting firms have installed new offices for their small business groups on Route 128 in the heart of entrepreneurs' country.

Accountants often are unfairly maligned—especially after the fallout of the Enron–Arthur Anderson case. The activities that accountants engage in have grown and no longer consist solely of counting numbers.[18] (Exhibit 3.3 outlines this trend for large accounting firms.) Accountants who are experienced as advisors to emerging companies can provide, in addition to audits and taxation, other valuable services. An experienced general business advisor can be invaluable in helping to think through strategy, in helping to find and raise debt and equity capital, in mergers and acquisitions, in locating directors, and in helping to balance business decisions with important personal needs and goals.

Exhibit 3.3 Areas of Growth for Large Accounting Firms

	1995 Revenues (Millions)	% Change Since 1990
Accounting and auditing	$6,004	+2.9%
Taxes	$3,197	+13.1%
Management-consulting services	$6,371	+117.7%

Source: Used with permission from "How Many Accountants Does It Take to Change an Industry?" As seen in the April 1, 1997, issue of *Inc.* magazine. Copyright ©1997 Gruner & Jahr USA Publishing. All rights reserved.

Consultants

The Decision.* Consultants are hired to solve particular problems and to fill gaps not filled by the management team. Many skilled consultants can be of invaluable assistance and a great source of "other people's resources." Advice needed can be quite technical and specific or quite general or far ranging. Problems and needs also vary widely, depending upon whether the venture is just starting up or is an existing business.

Start-ups usually require help with critical one-time tasks and decisions that will have lasting impact on the business. In a study of how consultants are used and their impact on venture formation, Karl Bayer of Germany's Institute for Systems and Innovation Research of the Fraunhofer Society interviewed 315 firms. He found that 96 used consultants and that consultants are employed by smaller but growing firms for the following reasons:

- To compensate for a lower level of professional experience
- To target a wide market segment (possibly to do market research for a consumer goods firm)
- To undertake projects that require a large start-up investment in equipment[19]

*The following is excerpted in part from David E. Gumpert and Jeffry A. Timmons, *The Encyclopedia of Small Business Resources* (New York: Harper & Row, 1982), pp. 48–51.

These tasks and decisions might include assessing business sites, evaluating lease and rental agreements, setting up record- and bookkeeping systems, finding business partners, obtaining capital, and formulating marketing plans.

Existing businesses face ongoing issues resulting from growth. Many of these issues—for example, market research, evaluating when and how to go about computerizing business tasks, whether to lease or buy major pieces of equipment, and whether to change inventory valuation methods can be involved—are so specialized that rarely is this expertise available on the management team.

While it is not always possible to pinpoint the exact nature of a problem (and sometimes simply an unbiased and fresh view is needed), a venture is usually well advised to try to determine the broad nature of its concern—such as whether it involves personnel, manufacturing, or marketing, for example. Mie-Yun Lee of BuyerZone.com offers helpful hints for establishing an effective consultation relationship: (1) Define, define, define—invest whatever time is necessary to define and communicate the expected outcome of the project; (2) when choosing a consultant, expect a long-term relationship as it takes time to get them up to speed on your business; and (3) don't assume that outsourcing is a magic bullet that relieves you of work. A high level of communication between your company and the outsourcing partner is critical to success.[20]

Conclusion

To grow a business requires an entrepreneur to grow as an individual. An important part of that personal growth is assessing your own strengths and weaknesses. But that very personal exercise has to be in context with the opportunity you are pursuing. By clearly defining the nature of the opportunity and the requisite skills and abilities required to exploit it, you identify the kind of people you'll need to achieve your goals. One of the strong messages of this chapter (and this book) is that great leadership is required to build a small company into a high-value venture. And great leaders build teams.

One of the advantages you have as a small business preparing to grow is that you can build a team and remain nimble. To do that often requires an expansive definition of the team concept. Suppliers, consultants, professional advisors, and both formal and informal networks, along with employees, constitute the team for the resource-conscious, highly flexible, and creative entrepreneurial company.

Notes

1. Howard H. Stevenson, Michael J. Roberts, and H. Irving Grousbeck, *New Business Ventures and the Entreprenuer* (Homewood, IL: Richard D. Irwin, Inc. 1985).

2. Ibid.

3. Emily Barker, "Start with Nothing," *Inc.*, Feb. 2002.

4. Howard H. Stevenson and William H. Sahlman, "How Small Companies Should Handle Advisors," in *The Entrepreneurial Venture* (Boston: Harvard Business School, 1999), p. 451. See also the *Harvard Business Review* reprint series "Boards of Directors: Part I" and "Board of Directors: Part II" (Boston: *Harvard Business Review*, 1976).

5. B. Honig and P. Davidsson, *The Role of Social and Human Capital Among Nascent Entrepreneurs* (Academy of Management Proceedings, 2001), pp. 1–7.

6. Stevenson and Sahlman, "How Small Companies Should Handle Advisors," in *The Entrepreneurial Venture*, p. 457.

7. R. A. Baron and G. D. Markman, "Beyond Social Capital: How Social Skills Can Enhance Entrepreneurs' Success," *Academy of Management Executive* 14, no. 1 (2000): pp. 106–17.

8. J. W. Lorsch, A. S. Zelleke, and K. Pick, "Unbalanced Boards," *Harvard Business Review* 79, no. 2 (2001): p. 28.

9. "Confessions of a Director: Hambro International's Art Spinner Says Most CEOs Don't Know How to Make Good Use of Boards. Here He Tells You How," *Inc.*, April 1991, p. 19.

10. D. E. Gumpert, "Tough Love: What You Really Want from Your Advisory Board" entreworld.org/content/entrebyline (2001).

11. Joseph Rosenstein, Albert V. Bruno, William D. Bygrave, and Natalie T. Taylor, "The CEO, Venture Capitalist, and the Board," *Journal of Business Venturing* 3, no. 2 (Spring 1988), pp. 99–113.

12. Ibid., pp. 99–100.

13. Used with permission from "Confessions of a Director." As seen in the April 1991 issue of *Inc.* magazine. Copyright © 1991 Gruner & Jahr USA Publishing. All rights reserved.

14. Hedgecock, Cathy, "The *Venture* Survey: Who Sits on Your Board?," *Venture* 6, no. 4 (April 1984), p. 32.

15. C. O. White and G. Gallop-Goodman, "Tap into Expert Input," *Black Enterprise* 30, no. 12 (2001), p. 47.

16. J. Adamec, "A Business Owner's Guide to Preventive Law" (1997), inc.com.

17. FindLaw, Inc. "Selecting an Attorney" (2000), findlaw.com.

18. J. Andresky Fraser, "How Many Accountants Does It Take to Change an Industry?" *Inc.*, April 1, 1997, inc.com.

19. Karl Bayer, "The Impact of Using Consultants During Venture Formation on Venture Performance," in *Frontiers of Entrepreneurship Research 1991*, ed. Neil H. Churchill et al. (Babson Park, MA: Babson College, 1991), pp. 298–99.

20. Mie-Yun Lee, "Finding the Right Consultant" (Feb. 2, 2000), buyerzone.com.

CHAPTER 4

VENTURE AND GROWTH FINANCING
THE ENTREPRENEUR'S ACHILLES' HEEL

"Happiness to an entrepreneur is a positive cash flow."
—FRED ADLER, VENTURE CAPITALIST

Finance can be arcane, complicated, and sometimes dangerous in the life of a business. But *entrepreneurial* finance, gathering the financial resources through value assessment and allocation for start-up or growth, differs from the more traditional corporate finance taught at business schools.

The Three Core Principles of Entrepreneurial Finance*

There are three core principles of entrepreneurial finance: (1) more cash is preferred to less cash, (2) cash sooner is preferred to cash later, and (3) less risky cash is preferred to more risky cash. While these principles seem simple enough, entrepreneurs, chief executive officers, and division managers often seem to ignore them. To many small business owners, financial analysis seems intimidating. Even management teams, comfortable with the financial issues, may not be adept at linking strate-

*This section is drawn from Jeffry A. Timmons, "Financial Management Breakthrough for Entrepreneurs."

75

gic and financial decisions to their companies' growth challenges and choices. Take, for example, the following predicaments:

- Reviewing the year-end results just handed to you by your accountant or chief financial officer, you see no surprises—except that the company loss is even larger than you had projected three months earlier. Therefore, for the fourth year in a row, you will have to walk into the boardroom and deliver bad news. A family-owned business since 1945, the company has survived and prospered with average annual sales growth of 17 percent. In fact, the company's market share has actually increased during recent years despite the losses. With the annual growth rate in the industry averaging less than 5 percent, your mature markets offer few opportunities for sustaining higher growth. How can this be happening? Where do you and your company go from here? How do you explain to the board that for four years you have increased sales and market share but produced losses? How will you propose to turn the situation around?

- During the past twenty years, your cable television company has experienced rapid growth through the expansion of existing properties and numerous acquisitions. At your company's peak, your net worth reached $25 million. The next decade of expansion was fueled by the high leverage common in the cable industry and valuations soared. Ten years later, your company had a market value in the *$500* million range. You had a mere $300 million in debt, and you owned 100 percent of the company. Just two years later, your *$200 million* net worth is an astonishing zero! Additionally, you now face a personally exhausting and financially punishing restructuring battle to survive; personal bankruptcy is a very real possibility. How could this happen? Can the company be salvaged?[1]

- At mid-decade, your company was the industry leader, meeting as well as exceeding your mid-decade business plan targets for annual sales, profitability, and new stores. Exceeding these targets while doubling sales and profitability each year has propelled your stock price from $15 at the initial public offering to the mid-$30s. Meanwhile, you still own a large chunk of the company. Then the shocker—at decade's end your company loses $78 million on just over $90 million in sales! The value of your stock plummets. A brutal restructuring follows in which the stock is stripped from the original management team, including you, and you are ousted from the company you founded and loved. Why did the company spin out of control? Why couldn't you as the founder have anticipated its demise? Could you have saved the company in time?

Financial Management Myopia: It Can't Happen to Me

All of these situations have three things in common. First, they are real companies and these events actually happened. Second, each of these companies was led by successful entrepreneurs who knew enough to prepare audited financial statements.* Third, in each example, the problems stemmed from financial management myopia, a combination of self-delusion and just plain not understanding the complex dynamics and interplay between financial management and business strategy. Why is this so?

Getting Beyond "Collect Early, Pay Late"

During our thirty-plus years as educators, authors, directors, founders, and investors in entrepreneurial companies, we have met a few thousand entrepreneurs and managers, including executives participating in an executive MBA program, MBA students, Kauffman Fellows, company founders, presidents, members of the Young Presidents' Organization, and the chief executive officers of middle-market companies. By their own admission, they felt uniformly uncomfortable, if not downright intimidated and terrified, by their lack of expertise in financial analysis and its relationship to management and strategy. No doubt about it, the vast majority of small business owners are strategically dis-

---

*Their outcomes have ranged from demise to moderate success, to radical downsizing followed by dramatic recovery, to still being in the midst of a turnaround.

advantaged by this lack of confidence in financial management. Beyond "collect early, pay late," there is precious little sophistication and enormous unease when it comes to these complex and dynamic financial interrelationships. Even good managers who are reveling in major sales increases and profit increases often fail to realize until it's too late the impact increased sales have on the cash flow required to finance the increased receivables and inventory.

The Spreadsheet Mirage

It is hard to imagine any entrepreneur who would not want ready answers to many financial vigilance questions. (See Exhibit 4.1.) Until now, however, getting the answers to these questions was a rarity. If the capacity and information are there to do the necessary analysis (and frequently they are not), it can take up to several weeks to get a response. In this era of spreadsheet mania, more often than not, the answers will come in the form of a lengthy report with innumerable scenarios, pages of numbers, backup exhibits, and possibly a stand-up presentation by a staff financial analyst, controller, or chief financial officer.

Yet, all too often the barrage of spreadsheet exhibits is really a *mirage*. What is missing? Traditional spreadsheets can only report and manipulate the data. The numbers may be there, the trends may be identified, but the connections and interdependencies between financial structure and business decisions inherent in key financial questions may be missed. As a result, gaining true insights and getting to creative alternatives and new solutions may be painfully slow, if not interminable. By themselves, spreadsheets cannot model the more complex financial and strategic interrelationships that entrepreneurs need to grasp. And for the board of directors, delays or failures to get this information can be disastrous. Such a weakness in financial know-how becomes life-threatening for entrepreneurs (such as those noted earlier) when it comes to anticipating the financial and risk-reward consequences of their business decisions. During a period of financial crisis, such a weakness can make an already dismal situation even worse.

Time and again, financially fluent and skillful entrepreneurs push what would otherwise be an average company toward greatness. What many entrepreneurs may fail to consider is the acumen of competitor

Exhibit 4.1 The Crux of It: Anticipation and Financial Vigilance

To avoid some of the greatest tar pits, entrepreneurs need answers to questions that link strategic business decisions to financial plans and choices. The crux of it is anticipation: What is *most likely* to happen? When? What can go right along the way? What can go wrong? What has to happen to achieve our business objectives and to increase or to preserve our options? Financially savvy entrepreneurs know that such questions trigger a process that can lead to creative solutions to their financial challenges and problems. At a practical level, financially astute entrepreneurs and managers maintain vigilance over numerous key strategic and financial questions:

- What are the *financial consequences* and implications of crucial business decisions such as pricing, volume, and policy changes affecting the balance sheet, income statement, and cash flow? How will these change over time?
- How can we measure and *monitor changes* in our financial strategy and structure from a management, not just a GAAP,* perspective?
- What does it mean to grow too fast in our industry? *How fast can we grow* without requiring outside debt or equity? How much capital is required if we increase or decrease our growth by *x* percent?
- What will happen to our *cash flow, profitability, return on assets, and shareholder equity* if we grow faster or slower by *x* percent?
- How much *capital* will this require? How much can be financed internally and how much will have to come from external sources? What is a reasonable mix of debt and equity?
- What if we are 20 percent less *profitable* than our plan calls for? Or 20 percent more profitable?
- What should be our *focus and priorities*? What are the cash flow and net income break-even points for each of our product lines? For our company? For our business unit?
- What about *our pricing, volume, and costs*? How sensitive is our cash flow and net income to increases or decreases in price, volume, or variable costs? What price-volume mix will enable us to achieve the same cash flow and net income?
- How will these changes in pricing, volume, and costs affect our *key financial ratios*, and how will we stack up against others in our industry? How will our lenders view this?
- *At each stage*—rapidly growing, stagnating, or mature company—how should we be thinking about these questions and issues?

*GAAP is an acronym for generally accepted accounting principles. Basic financial ratio formulas can be found at CPAclass.com/gaap.

CEOs. They will move faster, more nimbly, and with less risk because they understand the language and nuance of the finance world. Such adversaries enjoy a secret competitive weapon that can yield a decisive edge over less financially skilled entrepreneurs.

Critical Financing Issues

Exhibit 4.2 illustrates the central issues in entrepreneurial finance. These include the creation of value, how the value pie is sliced and divided among those who have a stake or have participated in the venture, and the handling of the risks inherent in the venture. Developing financing and fund-raising strategies, knowing what alternatives are available, and obtaining funding are tasks vital to the survival and success of most higher-potential ventures.

As a result, entrepreneurs face certain critical issues and problems that bear on the financing of entrepreneurial ventures:

- **Creating value.** Who are the constituencies for whom value must be created or added to achieve a positive cash flow and to develop harvest options?

Exhibit 4.2 Central Issues in Entrepreneurial Finance

- **Slicing the value pie:**
    - — How are deals, both for start-ups and for the purchases of existing ventures, structured and valued, and what are the critical tax consequences of different venture structures?
    - — What is the legal process, and what are the key issues involved in raising outside risk capital?
    - — How do entrepreneurs make effective presentations of their business plans to financing and other sources?
    - — What are some of the nastier pitfalls, minefields, and hazards that need to be anticipated, prepared for, and responded to?
    - — How critical and sensitive is timing in each of these areas?
- **Covering risk:**
    - — How much money is needed to start, acquire, or expand the business, and when, where, and how can it be obtained on acceptable terms?
    - — What sources of risk and venture capital financing—equity debt and other innovative types—are available, and how is appropriate financing negotiated and obtained?
    - — Who are the financial contacts and networks that need to be accessed and developed?
    - — How do successful entrepreneurs marshal the necessary financial resources and other financial equivalents to seize and execute opportunities? What pitfalls do they manage to avoid, and how? Can a staged approach to resource acquisition mitigate risk and increase return?

A clear understanding of the financing requirements is especially vital for new and emerging companies, because new ventures go through the torturous and heated competition for capital, compared to existing firms, both smaller and larger, that have a customer base and revenue stream. In the early going, new firms are gluttons for capital, yet are usually not very debt-worthy. To make matters worse, the faster they grow, the more gluttonous is their appetite for cash.

This phenomenon is best illustrated in Exhibit 4.3, where loss as a percentage of initial equity is plotted against time. The shaded area represents the cumulative cash flow of 157 companies from their inception.

For these firms, it took thirty months to achieve operating breakeven and seventy-five months (or going into the *seventh* year) to recover the initial equity. As can be seen from the illustration, *cash goes out for a long time before it starts to come in.* This phenomenon is at the heart of the financing challenges facing new and emerging companies.

Entrepreneurial Finance: The Owner's Perspective

There are both stark and subtle differences, both in theory and in practice, between entrepreneurial finance as practiced in higher-potential small firms and corporate or administrative finance, which usually occurs in larger publicly traded companies. Students and practitioners of entrepreneurial finance have always been dubious about the reliability and relevance of much of so-called modern finance theory.[2] High-potential small businesses need to focus their attention on key aspects of financial management. Consider the following:

- **Cash flow and cash.** Cash flow and cash are king and queen in entrepreneurial finance. Accrual-based accounting, earnings per share, or creative and aggressive use of the tax codes and rules of the Securities and Exchange Commission are not.
- **Time and timing.** Financing alternatives for the financial health of an enterprise are often more sensitive to, or vulnerable to, the time dimension. In entrepreneurial ventures, critical financing moves often have a shorter and more compressed time period, have a more rapidly changing optimum timing, and are subject to wider, more volatile swings from lows to highs and back.
- **Capital markets.** Capital markets for over 95 percent of growth financing for private entrepreneurial ventures are relatively imperfect, in that they are frequently inaccessible, unorganized, and often invisible. Virtually all the underlying characteristics and assumptions that dominate popular financial theories and models (such as the capital asset pricing model) simply do not apply, even up to the point of a public offering for a small company. In reality, there are so many

Exhibit 4.3 Initial Losses by Small New Ventures

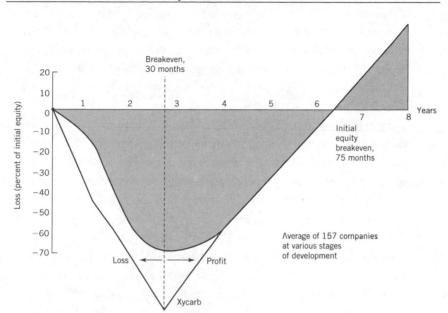

Source: Special appreciation is due to Bert Twaalfhoven, founder and chairman of Indivers, the Dutch firm that compiled this summary and that owns the firm on which the chart is based. Mr. Twaalfhoven was also a leader in the Class of 1954 at Harvard Business School and has been active in supporting the Entrepreneurial Management Interest Group and research efforts there.

and such significant information, knowledge, and market gaps and asymmetries that the rational, perfect market models suffer enormous limitations.

- **Emphasis.** While capital is one of the least important factors in the successful growth of higher-potential ventures, it is often a stumbling block for small businesses not used to finding resources for growth. When considering outside investors, you must seek not only the best deal but also the backer who will provide the most value in terms of know-how, wisdom, counsel, and help. Opt for the value added (beyond money), rather than just the best deal or share price.

- **Strategies for raising capital.** Strategies that optimize or maximize the amount of money raised can actually serve to increase risk in emerging companies, rather than lower it. Thus, the concept of "staged capital commitments," whereby money is invested for a three- to eighteen-month phase and is followed by subsequent commitments based on results and promise, is a prevalent practice among venture capitalists and other investors in higher-potential ventures. Similarly, wise entrepreneurs may refuse excess capital when the valuation is less attractive and when they believe that valuation will rise substantially.

- **Downside consequences.** Consequences of financial strategies and decisions are eminently more personal and emotional for the owners than for the management of large companies. The downside consequences for such entrepreneurs of running out of cash or failing are monumental and relatively catastrophic, since personal guarantees of bank or other loans are common.

- **Risk-reward relationships.** While the high-risk–high-reward and low-risk–low-reward relationship (a so-called law of economics and finance) works fairly well in efficient, mature, and relatively perfect capital markets (e.g., those with money market accounts, deposits in savings and loan institutions, widely held and traded stocks and bonds, and certificates of deposit), just the opposite occurs too regularly in entrepreneurial finance to permit much comfort with this law. Time and again, some of the most profitable, highest-return venture investments have been quite low-risk propositions from the outset. Yet the way the capital markets price these deals is just the reverse. The reasons are anchored in the second and third points noted above—timing and the asymmetries and imperfections of the capital markets for deals. Entrepreneurs or investors who create or recognize lower-risk, very-high-yield business propositions, before others jump on the Brink's truck, will defy the laws of economics and finance. By proving your business model and articulating growth strategies, you provide an exciting low-risk, high-return scenario.

- **Valuation methods.** Established company valuation methods, such as those based on discounted cash flow models used in Wall Street megadeals, seem to favor the seller, rather than the buyer, of private emerging entrepreneurial companies. A seller loves to see a recent MBA or investment banking firm alumnus show up with an HP calculator or the latest laptop personal computer and then proceed to develop "the ten-year discounted cash flow stream." The assumptions normally made and the mind-set behind them are irrelevant or grossly misleading for valuation of smaller private firms because of dynamic and erratic historical and prospective growth curves.

- **Conventional financial ratios.** Current financial ratios are misleading when applied to most private entrepreneurial companies. For one thing, entrepreneurs often own more than one company at once and move cash and assets from one to another. For example, an entrepreneur may own real estate and equipment in one entity and lease it to another company. Using different fiscal years compounds the difficulty of interpreting what the balance sheet really means and the possibilities for aggressive tax avoidance. Further, many of the most important value and equity builders in the business are off the balance sheet or are hidden assets: the excellent management team; the best scientist, technician, or designer; know-how and business relationships that cannot be bought or sold, let alone valued for the balance sheet.

- **Goals.** Creating value over the long term, rather than maximizing quarterly earnings, is a prevalent mind-set and strategy among highly successful entrepreneurs. Since profit is more than just the bottom line, financial strategies are geared to build value, often at the expense of short-term earnings. The growth required to build value often is heavily self-financed, thereby eroding possible accounting earnings.

Determining Capital Requirements

How much money does my venture need? When is it needed? How long will it last? Where and from whom can it be raised? How should this process be orchestrated and managed? The next two sections provide answers to the vital questions entrepreneurs should ask at any stage in the development of a company.

Financial Strategy Framework

The financial strategy framework shown in Exhibit 4.4 is a way to begin crafting financial and fund-raising strategies. The exhibit provides a flow and logic with which an otherwise confusing, if not befuddling, task can be attacked. *The opportunity leads and drives the business strategy, which in turn drives the financial requirements, the sources and deal structures, and the financial strategy.* (Again, unless and until this part of the exercise is well-defined, developing spreadsheets and "playing with the numbers" is just that—playing.)

If you have determined that your business has growth potential, you can begin to examine the financial requirements in terms of (1) asset needs (for expansion facilities, equipment, research and development, and other apparently one-time expenditures), and (2) operating needs (i.e., working capital for operations). This framework leaves ample room for crafting a financial strategy, for creatively identifying sources, for devising a fund-raising plan, and for structuring deals.

Each *fund-raising strategy*, along with its accompanying deal structure, commits the company to actions that incur actual and real-time costs and may enhance or inhibit future financing options. Similarly,

Exhibit 4.4 Financial Strategy Framework

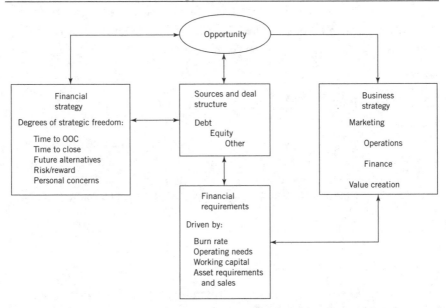

Source: This framework was developed for the Financing Entrepreneurial Ventures course at Babson College and has been used in the Entrepreneurial Finance course at the Harvard Business School.

each *source* has particular requirements and costs—both apparent and hidden—that carry implications for both financial strategy and financial requirements. The premise is that successful entrepreneurs are aware of potentially punishing situations, and that they are careful to "sweat the details" and proceed with a certain degree of wariness as they evaluate, select, negotiate, and craft business relationships with potential funding sources. In doing so, they are more likely to find the right sources, at the right time, and on the right terms and conditions. They are also more likely to avoid potential mismatches, costly sidetracking for the wrong sources, and the disastrous marriage to these sources that might follow.

Certain changes in the financial climate, such as the aftershocks felt after the stock-market crashes of October 1987 and March 2000, can cause repercussions across financial markets and institutions serving smaller companies. These take the form of greater caution by lenders and investors alike as they seek to increase their protection against risk. When the financial climate becomes harsher, an entrepreneur's capacity to devise financing strategies and to effectively deal with financing sources can be stretched to the limit and beyond. But it is exactly at a time like this that existing companies have a capital-markets advantage. Billions of risk-averse dollars retreat to the sidelines in angst. They can't make a return on the sideline but are too afraid to invest, unless they find an existing company with a reasonable track record and a desire to grow.

Free Cash Flow: Burn Rate, OOC, and TTC

The core concept in determining the external financing requirements of your venture is *free cash flow*. Three vital corollaries are the *burn rate*, time to *OOC*, and *TTC*. Let's define each of these concepts:

- Free cash flow, simply stated, is the amount of cash generated by your operating company after you have paid the government the required taxes and after you have invested in the current capital needs of the company. Historically, it has been considered as cash that is free to be returned to shareholders. For an entrepreneurial company, free cash flow is almost always used to grow.

Exhibit 4.5 Entrepreneur's Bargaining Power Based on Time to OOC

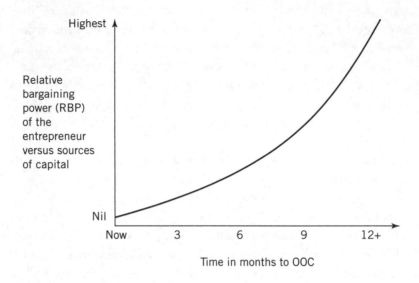

- Burn rate is the amount of your cash reserve that your company uses (burns!) each day.
- OOC, or "Out of Cash," should be the first thing an entrepreneur thinks about in the morning and the last at night. It is defined in terms of the days until the company is out of cash.
- TTC, or the time required to close the financing—and have the check clear!

The message is obvious: if you are out of cash in ninety days or less, you are at a major disadvantage. OOC even in six months is dangerously premature. But if you have a year or more, the options, terms, price, and agreements that you will be able to negotiate will improve significantly. The implication is clear: negotiate with the capital markets from a position of strength and you will get a better deal!

The cash flow generated by a company or project is defined as follows:

Earnings before interest and taxes (EBIT)

Less   Tax exposure (tax rate times EBIT)

Plus   Depreciation, amortization, and other noncash charges

Less   Increase in operating working capital

Less   Capital expenditures

Economists call this number free cash flow. The definition takes into account the benefits of investing, the income generated, and the cost of investing, the amount of investment in working capital and plant and equipment required to generate a given level of sales and net income.

This definition can be fruitfully refined further. Operating working capital is defined as:

Transactions cash balances

Plus   Accounts receivable

Plus   Inventory

Plus   Other operating current assets (e.g., prepaid expenses)

Less   Accounts payable

Less   Taxes payable

Less   Other operating current liabilities (e.g., accrued expenses)

Finally, this definition can be simplified:*

Earnings before interest but after taxes (EBIAT)

Less   Increase in net total operating capital (FA + WC)

where the increase in net total operating capital is defined as:

---

*For an exhaustive discussion of free cash flow see "Note on Free Cash Flow Valuation Models," HBS Case 9-288-023, pp. 2–3.

Increase in operating working capital

Plus   Increase in net fixed assets

Crafting Financial and Fund-Raising Strategies

Critical Variables

When financing is needed, a number of factors affect the availability of the various types of financing, and their suitability and cost:

- Accomplishments and performance to date. This is a big advantage for the existing small business. Investors will be impressed by:
    — Loyal customers, suppliers, and channel partners
    — A business model that yields profits and free cash flow
- Investor's perceived risk
- Industry and technology
- Venture upside potential and anticipated exit timing
- Venture anticipated growth rate
- Venture age and stage of development
- Investor's required rate of return or internal rate of return
- Amount of capital required and prior valuations of the venture
- Founders' goals regarding growth, control, liquidity, and harvesting
- Relative bargaining positions
- Investor's required terms and covenants

Certainly, numerous other factors—especially an investor's or lender's view of the quality of a business, the management team, and the growth opportunity—will also play a part in a decision to invest in or lend to a firm.

Generally speaking, a company's operations can be financed through debt and through some form of equity financing.* Moreover, it is generally believed that an existing business needs to obtain both equity and

---

*In addition to the purchase of common stock, equity financing is meant to include the purchase of both stock and subordinated debt, or subordinated debt with stock-conversion features or warrants to purchase stock.

debt financing if it is to have a sound financial foundation for growth without excessive dilution of the entrepreneur's equity.

Usually, short-term debt (i.e., debt incurred for one year or less) is used by a business for working capital and is repaid out of the proceeds of its sales. Longer-term borrowings (i.e., term loans of one to five years or long-term loans maturing in more than five years) are used for working capital and/or to finance the purchase of property or equipment that serve as collateral for the loan. Equity financing is used to fill the nonbankable gaps, preserve ownership, and lower the risk of loan defaults.

Even the underlying protection provided by a venture's assets used as loan collateral may be insufficient to obtain bank loans. Asset values can erode with time; in the absence of adequate equity capital and good management, they may provide little real loan security to a bank.*

An existing business seeking expansion capital or funds for a temporary use has a much easier job obtaining both debt and equity. Sources like banks, professional investors, and leasing and finance companies often will seek out such companies and regard them as important customers for secured and unsecured short-term loans or as good investment prospects. Furthermore, an existing and expanding business will find it easier to raise equity capital from private or institutional sources and to raise it on better terms than the start-up.

A key message here is that awareness of criteria used by various sources of financing—whether for debt, equity, or some combination of the two—that are available for a particular situation is central to devise a time-effective and cost-effective search for capital.

Financial Life Cycles

One useful way to begin the process of identifying equity financing alternatives, and when and if certain alternatives are available, is to consider what can be called the financial life cycle of firms. Exhibit 4.6 shows the types of capital available over time for different types of firms at different stages of development (i.e., as indicated by different sales

---

*The bank loan defaults by the real estate investment trusts (REITs) in 1975 and 1989–1991 are examples of the failure of assets to provide protection in the absence of sound management and adequate equity capital. The new millennium has seen a resurgence of REITs.

levels). It also summarizes, at different stages of development (research and development, start-up, early growth, rapid growth, and exit), the principal sources of risk capital and costs of risk capital.

As can be seen in the exhibit, sources have different preferences and practices, including how much money they will provide, when in a company's life cycle they will invest, and the cost of the capital or expected annual rate of return they are seeking. The available sources of capital

Exhibit 4.6 Financing Life Cycles

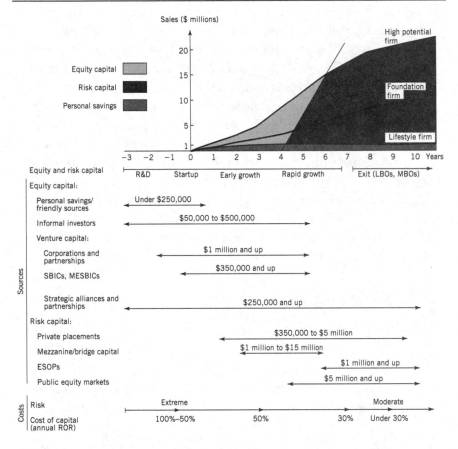

Source: Adapted and updated from the original by W. H. Wetzel, Jr., "The Cost of Availability of Credit and Risk Capital in New England," in *A Region's Struggling Savior: Small Business in New England*, ed. J. A. Timmons and D. E. Gumpert (Waltham, MA: Small Business Foundation of America, 1979), p. 175.

change dramatically for companies at different stages and rates of growth, and there will be variations in different parts of the country.

Thus, many sources of equity are not available until a company progresses beyond the earlier stages of its growth. Conversely, some of the sources available to early-stage companies, especially personal sources, friends, and other informal investors or angels, will be insufficient to meet the financing requirements generated in later stages, if the company continues to grow successfully.

Another key factor affecting the availability of financing is the upside potential of a company. Consider that of the three-million-plus new businesses of all kinds expected to be launched in the United States in 2004, probably 5 percent or less will achieve the growth and sales levels of high-potential firms. Foundation firms will total around 8–12 percent of all new firms, which will grow more slowly but exceed $1 million in sales and may grow to $5 million to $15 million. Remaining are the traditional, stable lifestyle firms. What have been called high-potential firms (those that grow rapidly and are likely to exceed $20 million to $25 million or more in sales) are strong prospects for a public offering and have the widest array of financing alternatives, including combinations of debt and equity and other alternatives (which are noted later on), while foundation firms have fewer, and lifestyle firms are limited to the personal resources of their founders and whatever net worth or collateral they can accumulate.

In general, investors believe the younger the company, the more risky the investment. This is a variation of the old saying in the venture capital business: The lemons ripen in two-and-a-half years, but the plums take seven or eight.

While the time line and dollar limits shown are only guidelines, they do reflect how these money sources view the riskiness, and thus the required rate of return, of companies at various stages of development.

Investor Preferences

It is important to realize that precise practices of investors or lenders may vary between individual investors or lenders in a given category and with the current market conditions, and may vary in different areas of the country.

Identifying realistic sources and developing a fund-raising strategy to tap them depend upon knowing what kinds of investments investors or lenders are seeking. While the stage, amount, and return guidelines noted in Exhibit 4.6 can help, doing the appropriate homework in advance on specific investor or lender preferences can save months of wild-goose chases and personal cash—while significantly increasing the odds of successfully raising funds on acceptable terms.

Conclusion

Cash isn't just king; it may be the whole royal family! And positive cash flow keeps the family happy. While seeking resources, especially financial resources, to build your company, more less-risky cash, sooner, is better than almost any alternative. At the heart of entrepreneurial finance is converting your vision of the company growth into quantified value creation, slicing the value pie and managing and covering financial risk. If you see the future clearly (or at least more clearly than the competitors), you'll be better able to determine capital requirements and craft financial and fund-raising strategies. Of course, value creation is ephemeral if not realized. In entrepreneurship, realization of value for the stakeholders is called "harvest" of a business. We will elaborate on this in later chapters.

Notes

1. For more detail, see Burton C. Hurlock and William A. Sahlman, "Star Cablevision Group: Harvesting in a Bull Market," HBS Case 293-036, Harvard Business School, September 17, 1992.

2. See Paul A. Gompers and William A. Sahlman, *Entrepreneurial Finance* (New York: John Wiley & Sons, 2002).

CHAPTER 5

OBTAINING VENTURE AND GROWTH CAPITAL

"Money is like a sixth sense without which you cannot make a complete use of the other five."

—W. SOMERSET MAUGHAM, *OF HUMAN BONDAGE*

The Capital Markets Food Chain

Consider the capital markets for equity as a "food chain," whose participants have increasing appetites in terms of the deal size they want to acquire (Exhibit 5.1). This framework can be quite useful to small business owners to identify and appreciate the various sources of equity capital at various stages of your business's development, the amount of capital they typically provide, and the portion of the company and the share price you might expect, should your company eventually have an initial public offering (IPO) or trade sale.

In the bottom row of Exhibit 5.1, you can see the ultimate progression from R&D stage to IPO, wherein the capital markets are typically willing to pay $12–$18 per share for new issues of small companies. Obviously, these prices are lower when the so-called IPO window is tight or closed, as it was in 2000 through 2002. Prices for the few offerings (one to three per week versus fifty-plus per week in June 1996) are

Exhibit 5.1 The Capital Markets Food Chain for Entrepreneurial Ventures

Stage of Venture	R&D	Seed	Launch	High Growth
Company Enterprise Value at Stage	<$1M	$1M–$5M	>$1M–$50M+	>$100M+
Sources	Founders; high-net-worth individuals; FFF*, SBIR	FFF; angel funds; seed funds; SBIR	Venture capital series A, B, C . . . ; strategic partners; very-high-net-worth individuals; private equity	IPOs; strategic acquirers; private equity
Amount of Capital Invested	<$50K–$200K	$10K–$500K	$500K–$20M	$10M–$50M+
Percent Company Owned at IPO	10–25%	5–15%	40–60% by prior investors	15–25% by public
Share Price and Number†	$0.01–$0.50; 1–5M	$0.50–$1.00; 1–3M	$1.00–$8.00±; 5–10M	$12–$18+; 3–5M

*Friends, families, and fools.

†At post-IPO.

single digits, $5–$9 per share. In hot IPO periods, 1999 for instance, offering prices reached as high as $20 per share and more.

One of the toughest decisions for you and any partners is whether to give up equity, and implicitly control, in order to have a run at creating very significant value. In the row "% company owned at IPO," you can see that by the time a company goes public, you may have sold 70–80 percent, or more, of your equity.

In the remainder of this chapter, we will discuss these various equity sources and how to identify and deal with them. Exhibit 5.2 summarizes the recent venture capital food chain. In the first three rounds (series A, B, C), you can see that on average, the amount of capital invested was quite substantial: $5 million, $7.5 million, and $12 million. Note that the total number of shares will not equal 100 percent if you add the maximum equity all investors might acquire. If that did happen, previous rounds would be diluted. Also, the total number of shares outstanding and your total number of shares owned will increase as you sell more shares. That happens mostly because you will issue new stock. You may also enact a stock split. The key is if you perform well, the share price (valuation of the company) will increase and your value at IPO can be substantial.

Cover Your Equity

One of the toughest trade-offs for any young company is to balance the need for growth capital with the preservation of equity. Holding on to as much as you can for as long as possible is generally good advice for

Exhibit 5.2 The Venture Capital Food Chain for Entrepreneurial Ventures

Venture Capital Series A, B, C, . . . (average size of round):

Round (Q4 2000)* { "A" @ $5M—Start-up
"B" @ $7.5M—Product development
"C"† @ $12M—Shipping product

*Valuations vary markedly by industry (e.g., $2x^5$ +).

†Valuations vary by region and venture capital cycle.

small business owners. The earlier the capital enters, regardless of the source, the more costly it is. Creative bootstrapping strategies can be great preservers of equity, as long as such parsimony does not slow down the venture's progress—a problem with many small businesses.

There are three central issues to consider when beginning to think about obtaining risk capital: (1) Does the venture need outside equity capital? (2) Do the founders want outside equity capital? (3) Who should invest? Although these considerations should be the focus of your management team, it is also important to remember that a smaller percentage of a larger pie is preferred to a larger percentage of a smaller pie. Or as one entrepreneur stated, "I would rather have a piece of a watermelon than a whole raisin."[1]

After reviewing the venture opportunity screening exercises and the free-cash-flow equations (including OOC, TTC, and breakeven), it will be easier to assess the need for additional capital. Deciding whether the capital infusion will be debt or equity is situation specific, and it may be helpful to be aware of the trade-offs involved. In the majority of the high-technology early-stage companies, some equity investment is normally needed to fund research and development, prototype development and product marketing, launch, and early losses.

Once your *need* for additional capital has been identified and quantified, you and your management team must consider the desirability of an equity investment. Bootstrapping continues to be an attractive source of financing. For instance, *Inc.* magazine suggested that entrepreneurs in certain industries "tap vendors"[2] by getting them to extend credit.

Other entrepreneurs interviewed by *Inc.* recommended quick payments from customers.[3] For instance, one entrepreneur, Rebecca McKenna, built a software firm from scratch that did $8 million in sales in 2001 with customers in the health-care industry. The robust economic benefits to her customers justified a 25 percent advance payment with each signed contract. This up-front cash has been a major source for her bootstrap financing. These options, and others, exist if your management team members feel that a loss of equity would adversely impact the company and their ability to manage it effectively. An equity investment requires that the management team firmly believe that investors can and will add value to the venture. With this conviction, your team can begin to identify those investors who bring expertise to the venture. Cash flow versus required rate of return is an important aspect of the "equity versus other" financing decision.

Deciding *who* should invest is a process, more than a decision. Your management team has a number of sources to consider. There are both informal and formal investors, private and public markets. The single most important criterion for selecting investors is what they can contribute to the value of your venture—beyond just funding. Angels or wealthy individuals are often sought because the amount needed may be less than the minimum investment required by formal investors (i.e., venture capitalists and private placements). Whether a venture capitalist would be interested in investing can be determined by the amount needed and the required rate of return expected.

Yet, small business owners should be cautioned that only a small percent of the companies seeking private equity actually wind up getting it at the end of the process. Additionally, the fees due the investment bankers and attorneys involved in writing up the prospectus and other legal documents must be paid whether or not your company raises capital.

Angels and Informal Investors

Who They Are

Wealthy individuals are probably the single most important source of capital for start-up and emerging businesses in America today.[4] To meet accreditation standards, angel investors are required by the Securities and Exchange Commission to have assets of at least $1 million.[5] According to the Center for Venture Research at the University of New Hampshire, there are approximately 400,000 active angels in the United States. In 2000, as tech stocks sank, U.S. angels invested an estimated $30 billion in start-up financing, compared with about $50 billion by venture capitalists.[6]

New Hampshire's Bill Wetzel has found these angels are mainly American self-made entrepreneur millionaires. They have substantial business and financial experience and are likely to be in their forties or fifties. They are also well educated; 95 percent hold college degrees from four-year colleges, and 51 percent have graduate degrees. Of the graduate degrees, 44 percent are in a technical field and 35 percent are in business or economics. According to Scott Peters, cofounder and co-CEO of AngelSociety, 96 percent of angels are men. One growing movement to involve female entrepreneurs and investors is Springboard, a not-for-profit organization that organizes a series of meetings with venture capitalists. Springboard venture capital forums in the United States have showcased more than two hundred companies and helped raise nearly $600 million in 2000 and 2001.

Because the typical angel will invest from $10,000 to $250,000 in any one deal, informal investors are particularly appropriate for the following:[7]

- Ventures with capital requirements of between $50,000 and $500,000
- Ventures with sales of $1–$2 million and the potential for $20 million within five to ten years of the equity investment.
- Small, established, privately held ventures with sales and profit growth of 10–20 percent per year. This is not rapid enough to be attractive to a professional investor, such as a venture capital firm, but can be attractive to angels.
- Companies who project high levels of FCF within three to five years

These investors may invest alone or in syndication with other wealthy individuals, may demand considerable equity for their interests, or may try to dominate ventures. They also can get very impatient when sales and profits do not grow as they expected.

Usually, these informal investors will be knowledgeable and experienced in the market and technology areas in which they invest. If the right angel is found, he or she will add a lot more to a business than just money. As an advisor or director, his or her savvy, know-how, and contacts that come from having "made it" can be far more valuable than the $10,000–$250,000 invested. Generally, the evaluations of potential investments by such wealthy investors tend to be less thorough than those undertaken by organized venture capital groups, and such noneconomic factors as the desire to be involved with entrepreneurship may be important to their investment decisions. And in fact, there is a clear geographic bias of a one-hour radius of the investors to the venture's location. A wealthy individual, for example, may want to help build businesses in his or her community.

Finding Informal Investors

Finding these backers is not easy. One expert noted: "Informal investors, essentially individuals of means and successful entrepreneurs, are a diverse and dispersed group with a preference for anonymity. Creative techniques are required to identify and reach them."[8] The Internet has provided small business owners with an effective method of locating such investors. Formal sources like Garage Technology Ventures (garage.com), Business Partners (businesspartners.com), and PrivateInvestor.com provide invaluable advice, assistance, and information regarding potential investors and help forge the link between investors and small business owners seeking capital. Specialized assistance for women include womenangels.net and the Center for Women and Enterprise (cweboston.org).

Invariably, financial backers are also found by tapping a small business owner's own network of business associates and other contacts. Other successful entrepreneurs know them, as do many tax attorneys, accountants, bankers, and other professionals. Apart from serendipity, the best way to find informal investors is to seek referrals from attorneys, accountants, business associates, university faculty, and entrepreneurs who deal with new ventures and are likely to know such people. Because such investors learn of investment opportunities from their business associates, fellow entrepreneurs, and friends, and because many informal investors invest together, more or less regularly, in a number of new venture situations, one informal investor contact can lead the entrepreneur to contacts with others.

In most larger cities, law firms and private placement firms syndicate investment packages as Regulation D offerings to networks of private investors. They may raise from several hundred thousand dollars to several million. Directories of these firms are published annually by *Venture* and discussed in other magazines such as *Inc.* Articles on angel investors can also be found in *Forbes, Fortune, Wall Street Journal* (WSJ Start-up.com), *Business Week, Red Herring,* and *Wired* and at their respective websites.

Contacting Investors

Obtain permission to use the name of the person making a referral when contacting the prospective investor. A meeting with the potential investor can then be arranged. At this meeting, you must make a concise presentation of the key features of the proposed venture by finding answers to the following questions:

- What is the market opportunity?
- Why is it compelling?
- How will/does the business make money?
- Why is this the right team at the right time?
- How, as an investor, does one exit the investment?

It is noteworthy that in this era following the crash of the dot-coms, investors throughout the capital markets food chain are returning to these fundamental basics for evaluating potential deals.

However, we recommend that you avoid meeting with more than one informal investor at the same time. It is unnecessary to hear negative viewpoints raised by one investor to be reinforced by another. It is also easier to deal with negative reactions and questions from only one investor at a time. Like a wolf on the hunt, if you isolate one target "prey" and then concentrate on closure, you will surely increase the odds of success.

Whether or not the outcome is continued investment interest, you need to try to obtain the names of other potential investors from this meeting. If this can be done, you will develop a growing list and will find your way into one or more networks of informal investors. If the outcome is positive, often the participation of one investor who is knowledgeable about the product and its market will trigger the participation of others.

Evaluation Process

An informal investor will want to review your business plan, meet your management team, and get to know your business by talking to employees, customers, vendors, and bankers. The investor will conduct background checks on your venture, usually through someone who knows both you and the product. The process is not dissimilar to the due diligence of the professional investors (see pages 120–21) but may be less formal and structured. If given a choice, you would be wise to select an informal investor who can add knowledge, wisdom, and networks as an advisor and whose objectives are consistent with your own.

The Decision

If the investor decides to go forward, he or she will have some sort of investment agreement drafted by an attorney. This agreement may be somewhat simpler than those used by professional investors, such as venture capital firms.

Most likely, the investment agreement with an informal investor will include some form of a "put," whereby the investor has the right to require the venture to repurchase his or her stock after a specified number of years at a specified price. If the venture is not harvested, this put will provide an investor with a guaranteed cash return.

Venture Capital: Gold Mines and Tar Pits

There are only two classes of investors in private companies: value-added investors, and all the rest. If all you receive from an investor, especially a venture capitalist or a substantial private investor, is money, then you may not be getting much of a bargain at all. One of the keys to raising risk capital is to seek investors who will truly add value to the venture well beyond the money. Research and practice show that investors may add or detract value in a company. Therefore, carefully screening potential investors to determine how specifically they might fill in some gaps in your know-how and networks can yield significant results. Adding key management, new customers or suppliers, or referring additional investment are basic ways to add value.

Private investors should provide critical assistance like introducing the founder to other private investors, to executives (who become investors and provide help in sales and strategic alliances), to the appropriate legal and accounting firms; serving as a sounding board in crafting and negotiating early rounds of investments; and identifying potential directors and other advisors familiar with the technology and relationships with foreign investors and cross-cultural strategic alliances.

Numerous other examples exist of investors being instrumental in opening doors to key accounts and vendors that otherwise might not take a new company very seriously. They may also provide valuable help in such tasks as negotiating OEM agreements, licensing or royalty agreements, making key contacts with banks and leasing companies, finding key people to build the team, and helping to revise or to craft a strategy. Norwest Venture Partners brought in Ashley Stephenson to grow a portfolio company and then backed him in a second venture. "Most venture capitalists have a short list of first-class players. Those are the horses you back," says Norwest partner Ernie Parizeau.

It is always tempting for a small business owner in need of cash to go after the money that is available, rather than wait for the value-added investor. These quick solutions to the cash problem usually come back to haunt the venture.

What Is Venture Capital?*

The word *venture* suggests that this type of capital involves a degree of risk and even something of a gamble. Specifically, as defined by Helen

*Unless otherwise noted, this section is drawn from William D. Bygrave and Jeffry A. Timmons, *Venture Capital at the Crossroads* (Boston: Harvard Business School Press, 1992), pp. 13–14. Copyright © 1992 by William D. Bygrave and Jeffry A. Timmons.

Soussou, "the venture capital industry supplies capital and other resources to entrepreneurs in business with high growth potential in hopes of achieving a high rate of return on invested funds."[9] The whole investing process involves many stages, which are represented in Exhibit 5.3. Throughout the investing process, venture capital firms seek to add value in several ways: identifying and evaluating business opportunities, including management, entry, or growth strategies; negotiating and closing the investment; tracking and coaching the company; providing technical and management assistance; and attracting additional capital, directors, management, suppliers, and other key stakeholders and resources. The process begins with the conception of a target investment opportunity or class of opportunities, which leads to a written proposal or prospectus to raise a venture capital fund. Once the money is raised, the value creation process moves from generating deals to crafting and executing harvest strategies and back to raising another fund. The process usually takes up to ten years to unfold, but exceptions in both directions often occur.

The Venture Capital Industry Pre-1990

Although the roots of venture capital can be traced from investments made by wealthy families in the 1920s and 1930s, most industry observers credit Ralph E. Flanders, then president of the Federal Reserve Bank of Boston, with the idea. In 1946, Flanders joined a top-ranked team to found American Research and Development Corporation, the first firm, as opposed to individuals, to provide risk capital for new and rapidly growing firms (most of which were manufacturing and technology oriented).

Despite the success of American Research and Development, the venture capital industry did not experience a growth spurt until the 1980s, when the industry "went ballistic." See Exhibit 5.4 for the U. S. capital commitments between 1969 and 2003. Before 1980, venture capital investing activities could be called dormant; just $460 million was invested in 375 companies in 1979. By 1987, the industry had ballooned to more than 700 venture capital firms, which invested $3.94 billion in 1,729 portfolio companies. The sleepy, cottage industry of

Exhibit 5.3 Classic Venture Capital Investing Process

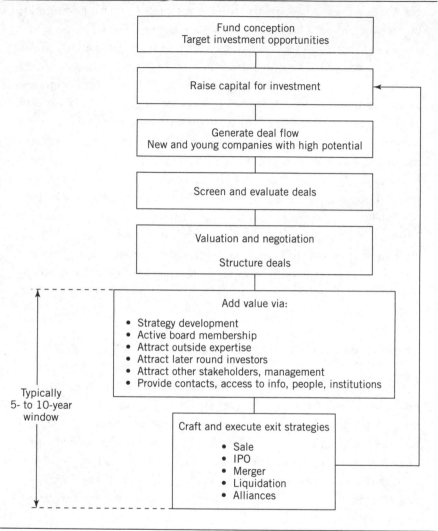

Fund conception
Target investment opportunities

Raise capital for investment

Generate deal flow
New and young companies with high potential

Screen and evaluate deals

Valuation and negotiation

Structure deals

Add value via:

- Strategy development
- Active board membership
- Attract outside expertise
- Attract later round investors
- Attract other stakeholders, management
- Provide contacts, access to info, people, institutions

Typically
5- to 10-year
window

Craft and execute exit strategies

- Sale
- IPO
- Merger
- Liquidation
- Alliances

Source: William D. Bygrave and Jeffry A. Timmons, *Venture Capital at the Crossroads* (Boston: Harvard Business School Press, 1992), Figure 1-4.

the 1970s was transformed into a vibrant, at times frenetic, occasionally myopic, and dynamic market for private risk and equity capital in the 1980s. According to Michael Vachon, "After shrinking by an average of 25 percent a year for four years, new venture capital raised in

1992 more than doubled over 1991."[10] Yet industry observers attributed the increase to "repeat fund raisers assembling partnerships of more than $100 million."[11]

The Booming 1990s

As one can see in Exhibit 5.5, the industry experienced an eightfold increase in the 1990s. While the absolute dollars committed and invested by 2000 were huge, the rate of increase in the 1980s was much greater, $1 billion in 1979 and $31 billion in 1989.

By 2001, not only had the commitments changed, but a new structure was also emerging, increasingly specialized and focused. Exhibit 5.6 summarizes some of the important changes in the industry, which have implications for small business owners seeking money and for those investing it. Several major structural trends that emerged at the end of

Exhibit 5.4 U.S. Commitments (1969–2003)

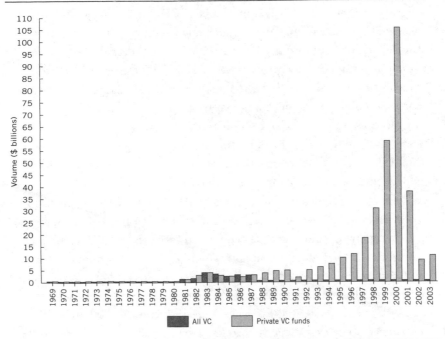

Source: Thomson Financial, May 2004.

Exhibit 5.5 Total Venture Capital Under Management

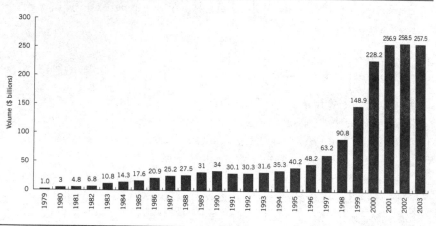

Source: Thomson Financial, May 2004.

the 1980s continued through the 1990s: (1) The average fund size grew larger and larger; megafunds in excess of $500 million accounted for nearly 80 percent of all capital under management. High-performing funds like Spectrum Equity Partners and Weston-Presidio (whose first fund just seven years earlier was in the $100–$200 million range) closed funds in 2000 well over $1 billion. (2) The average size of investments correspondingly grew much larger as well. Unheard of previously, start-up and early rounds of $20 million, $40 million, and even $80 million were plunked down in the dot-com and telecom feeding frenzy of the late 1990s. (3) The specialization pattern that began in the 1980s expanded to mainstream and megafunds.

The one significant trend that was reversed in the 1990s is especially good news for growth-minded companies. During the 1990s, start-up and early-stage funds experienced a major rebirth as opportunities in the Internet, software, information technology and telecommunications, and networking exploded. But the dot-com implosion left a lot of cash on the sideline. Many funds are looking to existing firms with track records and the potential for scale. Indeed, between 2000 and 2003 a majority of venture capital went to growth companies rather than start-up firms.[12]

Exhibit 5.6 New Heterogeneous Structure of the Venture Capital Market

	Megafunds	Mainstream	Second Tier	Specialists and Niche Funds	Corporate Financial and Corporate Industrial
Estimated Number and Type (2000)	106—Predominantly private, independent funds	76—Predominantly private and independent; some large institutional SBICs and corporate funds	455—Mostly SBICs; some private independent funds	87—Private, independent	114
Size of Funds Under Management	More than $500 million	$250–$499 million	Less than $250 million	$25–$50 million	$50–$100 million +
Typical Investment	Series B, C, . . . : $5–$25 million +	Series A, B, C, . . . : $1–$10 million	Series A, B: $500,000–$5 million	Series A, B: $500,000–$2 million	Series A, B, C, . . . : $1–$25 million
Stage of Investment	Later expansion, LBOs, start-ups	Later expansion, LBOs, some start-ups; mezzanine	Later stages; few start-ups; specialized areas	Seed and start-up; technology or market focus	Later
Strategic Focus	Technology; national and international markets; capital gains; broad focus	Technology and manufacturing; national and regional markets; capital gains; more specialized focus	Eclectic—more regional than national; capital gains, current income; service business	High-technology national and international links; "feeder funds," capital gains	Windows on technology; direct investment in new markets and suppliers; diversification; strategic partners; capital gains

(continued)

Exhibit 5.6 New Heterogeneous Structure of the Venture Capital Market (continued)

	Megafunds	Mainstream	Second Tier	Specialists and Niche Funds	Corporate Financial and Corporate Industrial
Balance of Equity and Debt	Predominantly equity	Predominantly equity; convertible preferred	Predominantly debt (about 91 SBICs principally equity)	Predominantly equity	Mixed
Principal Sources of Capital	Mature national and international institutions; own funds; insurance company and pension funds; institutions and wealthy individuals; foreign corporation and pension funds; universities	Mature national and international institutions; own funds; insurance company and pension funds; institutions and wealthy individuals; foreign corporation and pension funds; universities	Wealthy individuals; some smaller institutions	Institutions and foreign companies; wealthy individuals	Internal funds
Main Investing Role	Active lead or colead; frequent syndications; board seat	Less investing with some solo investing	Initial or lead investor; outreach; shirtsleeves involvement	Later stages, rarely start-ups; direct investor in funds and portfolio companies	Conduit to an array of capital markets for debt and equity

Source: 2001 National Venture Capital Association Yearbook.

Note: Target rates of return vary considerably, depending on stage and market conditions. Seed and start-up investors may seek compounded after-tax rates of return in excess of 50–100 percent; in mature, later stage investments, they may seek returns in the 30–40 percent range. The rule of thumb of realizing gains of five to ten times the original investment in five to ten years is a common investor expectation.

Venture Capital Industry

Beyond the Crash of 2000: The Venture Capital Cycle Repeats Itself

The crash of the NASDAQ began in March 2000, resulting in more than a 60 percent drop in value by late summer 2001. This major crash in equity values began a shakeout and downturn in the private equity and public stock markets whose repercussions and consequences are still impacting the venture and growth capital marketplace. Typical of the dot-com meltdown, many high-flying companies went public in 1998 and 1999 at high prices, saw their values soar beyond $150 to $200 per share, and then came plummeting to low single-digit prices. Take Sycamore Networks, which went public in October 1999 at $38 per share, rocketed to nearly $200 in the first week, and was trading at under $6 per share through most of 2003. The list of dot-coms that went totally bankrupt (such as webvan.com, the home delivery grocery firm) is significant.

Similarly, beginning in the late summer of 2000, many young telecommunications companies saw their stocks begin to decline rapidly, losing 90 percent or more of their value in less than a year. These downdrafts swept the entire venture capital and private equity markets. By mid-2001, the amount of money being invested had dropped by half from the record year of 2000, and valuations plummeted. Down rounds—investing at a lower price than the previous round—were truly the catch of the day. Not since the periods 1969–1974 and 1989–1993 have entrepreneurs experienced such a downturn.

To illustrate the consequences for small business owners and investors alike, in 2001 as companies burned through their invested capital and faced follow-on round of financing, the valuations were sagging painfully. Even companies performing on plan were seeing share prices 15–30 percent below the previous round a year or eighteen months earlier. Where performance lagged milestones in the business plan, the down round could be 50 percent or more below the previous financing valuation. To make matters worse for entrepreneurs, the investing pace slowed significantly. Due diligence on companies was completed in forty-five days or less during the binge of 1998–1999. By 2002 investors reported a six- to eight-month due diligence phase, which would be very close to the historical norm experienced prior to the feeding frenzy.

The stark reality of all this, which is summarized in Exhibits 5.4 and 5.5, is that the venture capital cycle—much like real estate—seems to repeat itself. Scarcity of capital leads to high returns that attract an over-abundance of new capital, which drives returns down. The new millennium welcomed the real "Y2K problem": the meltdown side of the venture capital and private equity markets repeated the 1969–1974 and 1989–1993 pattern.

The Venture Capital Process

Exhibit 5.7 represents the core activities of the venture capital process. At the heart of this dynamic flow is the collision of entrepreneurs, opportunities, investors, and capital.[13] Because the venture capitalist brings, in addition to money, experience, networks, and industry contacts, a professional venture capitalist can be very attractive to a new venture. Moreover, a venture capital firm has deep pockets and contacts with other groups that can facilitate the raising of money as the venture develops.

The venture capital process occurs in the context of mostly private, quite imperfect capital markets for new, emerging, and middle-market companies (i.e., those companies with $5 million to $200 million in sales). The availability and cost of this capital depend on a number of factors:

- Perceived risk, in view of the quality of the management team and the opportunity
- Industry, market, attractiveness of the technology, and fit
- Upside potential and downside exposure
- Anticipated growth rate
- Age and stage of development
- Amount of capital required
- Founders' goals for growth, control, liquidity, and harvest

Exhibit 5.7 Flows of Venture Capital

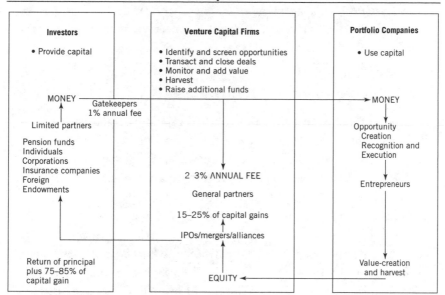

Investors	Venture Capital Firms	Portfolio Companies
• Provide capital	• Identify and screen opportunities • Transact and close deals • Monitor and add value • Harvest • Raise additional funds	• Use capital

Source: William D. Bygrave and Jeffry A. Timmons, *Venture Capital at the Crossroads* (Boston: Harvard Business School Press, 1992), Figure 1-3.

- Fit with investors' goals and strategy
- Relative bargaining positions of investors and founders given the capital markets at the time

Further, a small business owner may give up 15–75 percent of his or her equity for seed/start-up financing. Thus, after several rounds of venture financing have been completed, a small business owner entrepreneur may own no more than 10–20 percent of the venture.

It is the venture capitalists' stringent criteria for their investments that limit the number of companies receiving venture capital money. Venture capital investors look for ventures with very high growth potential where they can quintuple their investment in five years; they place a very high premium on the quality of management in a venture; and they like to see a management team with complementary business skills headed by someone who has previous entrepreneurial or profit-and-loss (P&L) management experience. In fact, these investors are searching for the "superdeal." Superdeals meet the investment criteria outlined in Exhibit 5.8.

Identifying Venture Capital Investors

Venture capital firms have an established capital base and professional management. Their investment policies cover a range of preferences in investment size and the maturity, location, and industry of a venture. Capital for these investments can be provided by one or more wealthy families, one or more financial institutions (e.g., insurance companies or pension funds), and wealthy individuals. Most are organized as limited partnerships, in which the fund managers are the general partners and the investors are the limited partners. Today, most of these funds prefer to invest from $2 million to $5 million or more per round, although some of the smaller funds will invest less. Some of the so-called megafunds (comprising more than $500 million) do not consider investments of less than $5 million to $10 million. The investigation and evaluation of potential investments by venture capital corporations and partnerships are thorough and professional. Most of their investments are in high-technology businesses, but a good number will consider investments in other areas.

Sources and Guides. If you are searching for a venture capital investor, a good place to start is *Pratt's Guide to Venture Capital Sources* (published by Venture Economics), the VentureOne website (venture-one.com), and the directory published at the PricewaterhouseCoopers MoneyTree Survey website (pwcmoneytree.com).

Because venture capital firms receive thousands of proposals every year, their first screen as to whether they will pay any attention to the business plan is whether it comes from a "warm" referral. If you mail your plans unsolicited to a number of firms, you will be very lucky if one even acknowledges that you sent them a plan, let alone reads it and considers it as a deal worth investigating further. Therefore, you need to find a "warm" referral to each venture capital firm you plan to contact. Small business owners can seek referrals from accountants, law-

Exhibit 5.8 Characteristics of the Classic Superdeal from the Investor's Perspective

Mission
- Bring scale to a highly profitable company that can become the industry-dominant, market-leading company
- Go public or merge within four to seven years at a high price/earnings (P/E) multiple or sell to a larger company at a high P/E
- Complete management team
- Led by industry "superstar"
- Possess proven entrepreneurial, general management, and P&L experience in the business
- Have leading innovator or technologies/marketing head
- Possess complementary and compatible skills
- Have unusual tenacity, imagination, and commitment
- Possess reputation for high integrity

Proprietary Product or Service
- Has significant competitive lead and "unfair" and sustainable or defensible advantages
- Has product or service with high value-added properties resulting in early payback to user
- Has or can gain exclusive contractual or legal rights
- Large, robust, and sustainable business model
- Will accommodate a $100 million entrant in five years
- Has sales currently at $200 million, or more, and growing at more than 25 percent per year
- Has no dominant competitor now
- Has clearly identified customers and distribution channels
- Possesses forgiving and rewarding economics, such as:
    —gross margins of 40–50 percent, or more
    —10 percent or more profit after tax
    —early positive cash flow and break-even sales

Deal Valuation and ROR
- Has "digestible" first-round capital requirements (i.e., greater than $1 million and less than $10 million)
- Able to return ten times original investment in five years at P/E of fifteen times or more
- Has possibility of additional rounds of financing at substantial markup
- Has antidilution and IPO subscription rights and other identifiable harvest/liquidity options

Source: Jeffry A. Timmons with Leonard E. Smollen and Alexander L. M. Dingee Jr., *New Venture Creation*, 3rd ed., (Homewood, IL: Richard D. Irwin, Inc. 1990).

yers, investment and commercial bankers, business school professors, and businesspeople who are knowledgeable about professional investors.

What to Look For. You are well advised to screen prospective investors to determine their appetites for the growth stage, industry, technology, and capital requirements proposed. The Pricewaterhouse-Coopers MoneyTree Survey is particularly useful in that it allows you to sort venture capital funds by region and industry focus, with links to the funds' home pages. Most of the firms give explicit definitions of what types of deals they are interested in, as well as an overview of other companies in which they have invested. Thus, you can identify venture capital firms that might provide value-added benefits (e.g., the fund may have invested in some potential suppliers or customers, meaning they can network you to these important firms).

Studying the venture capital firm's website can help you answer a number of questions—for example, do they have money to invest, are they actively seeking deals, and do they have the time and people to investigate new deals? Depending on its size and investment strategy, a fund that is a year or two old will generally be in an active investing mode.

Growth-minded entrepreneurs need to seek investors who (1) are considering new financing proposals and can provide the required level of capital; (2) are interested in companies at the particular stage of growth; (3) understand and have a preference for investments in the particular industry (i.e., market, product, technology, or service focus); (4) can provide good business advice, moral support, and contacts in the business and financial community; (5) are reputable, fair, and ethical and with whom the small business owner gets along; and (6) have successful track records of ten years or more of advising and building smaller companies into larger ones.[14]

You can expect a number of value-added services from an investor. Ideally, the investor should define his or her role as a coach—thoroughly involved, but not a player. In terms of support, investors should have both patience and bravery. You should be able to go to the investor when you need a sounding board, counseling, or an objective, detached perspective. Investors should be helpful with future negotiations, financing, and private and public offerings, as well as in relationship building with key contacts.

Warning Signs. There are also some things to be wary of in finding investors. These warning signs are worth avoiding unless an entrepreneur is so desperate that he or she has no real alternatives:

- **Attitude.** If you cannot get through to a general partner in an investment firm and keep getting handed off to a junior associate, or if the investor thinks he or she can run the business better than you or your management team, you will probably want to look elsewhere.
- **Overcommitment.** Lead investors who indicate they will be active directors but who also sit on the boards of six to eight other start-up and early-stage companies, or are in the midst of raising money for a new fund, probably will have less time to devote to your firm.
- **Inexperience.** You can't necessarily rely on a venture capitalist who has an MBA; is under thirty years of age; has worked only on Wall Street or as a consultant; lacks operating, hands-on experience in new and growing companies; and has a predominantly financial focus.
- **Unfavorable reputation.** Look out for funds that have a reputation for early and frequent replacement of the founders or those where over one-fourth of the portfolio companies are in trouble or failing to meet projections in their business plans.
- **Predatory pricing.** During adverse capital markets (e.g., 1969–1974, 1988–1992, 2000–?), investors who unduly exploit these conditions by forcing large share price decreases in the new firms and punishing terms on prior investors do not make the best long-term financial partners.

How to Find Out. How do you learn about the reputation of the venture capital firm? Far and away the best source is the CEO or founders of prior investments. Besides the successful deals, ask for the names and phone numbers of CEOs they invested in whose results were only moderate to poor, and where they had to cope with significant adversity. Talking with these CEOs will reveal their underlying fairness, character, values, ethics, and potential as a financial partner, as well as how they practice their investing philosophies. It is always interesting to probe regarding the behavior at pricing meetings.

Dealing with Venture Capitalists*

It is important to keep in mind that venture capitalists see lots of proposals, sometimes one hundred or more a month. Typically, they invest in only one to three of these. The following suggestions may be helpful in working with them.

If possible, obtain a personal introduction from someone who is well known to the investors (a director or founder of one of their portfolio companies, a limited partner in their fund, a lawyer or accountant who has worked with them on deals) and who knows you well. After identifying the best targets, you should create a market for your company by having several prospects. Be vague about who else you are talking with. The problem is, you can end up with a rejection from everyone if the other firms know who was the first firm that turned you down. It is also much harder to get a yes than to get a no. And you can waste an enormous amount of time before receiving an answer.

When pushed by the investors to indicate what other firms/angels you are talking to, simply put it this way: "All our advisors believe that information is highly confidential to the company, and our team agrees. We are talking to other high-quality investors like you. The ones with the right chemistry who can make the biggest difference in our company, and are prepared to invest first, will be our partner. Once we have a term sheet and deal on the table, if you also want coinvestors we are more than happy to share these other investors' names." Failing to take such a tack usually puts you in a quite adverse negotiating position.

Most investors who have serious interest will have some clear ideas about how to improve your strategy, product line, positioning, and a variety of other areas. This is one of the ways they can add value—if they are right. Consequently, you need to be prepared for them to take apart your business plan—and to put it back together again. They are likely to have their own format and their own financial models. Working with them on this is a good way to get to know them.

Never lie. As one entrepreneur put it, "You have to market the truth, but do not lie." Do not stop selling until the money is in the bank. Let

---

*The authors express appreciation to Mr. Thomas Huseby, of SeaPoint Ventures in Washington, for his valuable insights in the following two sections.

the facts speak for themselves. Be able to deliver on the claims, statements, and promises you make or imply in your business plan and presentations. Tom Huseby adds some final wisdom: "It's much harder than you ever thought it could be. You can last much longer than you ever thought you could. They have to do this for the rest of their lives!" Finally, never say no to an offer price. There is an old saying that your first offer may be your best offer.

Questions the Entrepreneur Can Ask

The investor presentation phase of the venture-capital-seeking process is demanding and pressing, which is appropriate for this high-stakes game. Venture capitalists have an enormous legal and fiduciary responsibility to their limited partners, not to mention their powerful self-interest. Therefore, they are thorough in their due diligence and questioning to assess the intelligence, integrity, nimbleness, and creativity of the entrepreneurial mind in action.

Once the presentation and question-and-answer session is complete, the management team can learn a great deal about the investors, and enhance their own credibility, by asking a few simple questions:

- Do you believe in our plan to bring scale to our business?
- Tell us what you think of our strategy, how we size up competition, and game plan. What have we missed? Whom have we missed?
- Are there competitors we have overlooked? How are we vulnerable, and how do we compete? What is the likely response of the major competitors?
- How would you change the way we are thinking about scaling the business and planning to seize the bigger opportunity?
- Is our team as strong as you would like? How would you improve this and when?
- Give us a sense of what you feel would be a fair range of value for our company if you invested *x* amount of dollars?

Their answers will reveal how much homework they have done and how knowledgeable they are about your industry, technology, competitors, and the like. This will provide robust insight as to whether and how they can truly add value to the venture. At the same time, you will get a better sense of their forthrightness and integrity: are they direct, straightforward, but not oblivious to the impact of their answers? Finally, these questions can send a very favorable message to investors: this management team is intelligent, open-minded, receptive, and self-confident enough to solicit our feedback and opinions, even though we may have opposing views.

Due Diligence: A Two-Way Street

It can take several weeks or even months to complete the due diligence on a company, although it can go much more quickly if the investors know you. The verification of facts, backgrounds, and reputations of key people, customer satisfaction and market estimates, technical capabilities of the product, proprietary rights, and so on, is a painstaking investigation for investors. They will want to talk with your directors, advisors, management team, key customers, and major suppliers. Make it as easy as possible for them by having very detailed résumés, lists of ten to twenty references (with phone numbers and addresses), including former customers, bankers, and vendors, who can attest to your accomplishments. Prepare extra copies of such material as published articles, reports, studies, market research, contracts, purchase orders, and technical specifications to support your claims.

One recent research project examined how eighty-six venture capital firms nationwide conducted their intensive due diligence. In order to evaluate the opportunity, management, risks, and competition, and to weigh the upside against the downside, firms spent from 40 to 400 hours, with the typical firm spending 120 hours. That is nearly three weeks of full-time effort. At the extreme, some firms engaged in twice as much due diligence.[15] Central to this investigation were careful checks of the management's references and verification of track record and capabilities.

While all this is going on, do your own due diligence on the venture fund. Ask for the names and phone numbers of some of their successful deals, some that did not work out, and the names of any presidents they ended up replacing. Who are their legal and accounting advisors? What footprints have they left in the sand, vis-à-vis their quality, reputation, and record in truly adding value to the companies in which they invest? Finally, the chemistry between the management team and the general partner that will have responsibility for the investment and, in all likelihood, a board seat is crucial. If you do not have a financial partner you respect and can work closely with, then you are likely to regret ever having accepted the money.

Other Equity Sources

Small Business Administration's 7(a) Guaranteed Business Loan Program[16]

Promoting small businesses by guaranteeing long-term loans, the Small Business Administration's 7(a) Guaranteed Business Loan Program has been supporting start-up and high-potential ventures since 1953. The 7(a) loan program provides 40,000 loans annually and is extensively a guarantee program. But under this program the Small Business Administration also makes direct loans to women, veterans of the armed forces, and minorities, as well as other small businesses. The program entails banks and certain nonbank lenders making loans that are then guaranteed by the SBA for 50–90 percent of each loan, with a maximum of $1 million. Eligible activities under 7(a) include acquisition of borrower-occupied real estate, fixed assets such as machinery and equipment, and working capital for items such as inventory or to meet cash-flow needs.[17]

SBA programs have a noteworthy effect on the economy and entrepreneurship. The $1 million guarantees, the largest of all the SBA programs, have helped many entrepreneurs start, stay in, expand, or purchase a business. According to the SBA, over 541,000 jobs were created by SBA borrowers in the year 2000, and the SBA helped create 2.3 million jobs—about 15 percent of all jobs created by small businesses between 1993 and 1998.

Small Business Investment Companies*

SBICs (small business investment companies) are licensed by the SBA and can obtain from it four dollars in debt-capital loans for each dollar

*This section is drawn from Jeffry A. Timmons, *Planning and Financing the New Venture* (Acton, MA: Brick House Publishing, 1990), pp. 49–50.

of private equity. The impact of SBICs is evidenced by the many major U.S. companies that received early financing from SBICs, including Intel, Apple Computer, Staples, Federal Express, Sun Microsystems, Sybase, Inc., Callaway Golf, and Outback Steakhouse.[18] The SBIC program was established in 1958 to address the need for venture capital by small emerging enterprises and to improve opportunities for growth.[19] One or more commercial banks, wealthy individuals, and the investing public generally supply an SBIC's equity capital. The benefit of the SBIC program is twofold: (1) small businesses that qualify for assistance from the SBIC program may receive equity capital, long-term loans, and expert management assistance; and (2) venture capitalists participating in the SBIC program can supplement their own private investment capital with funds borrowed at favorable rates through the federal government. According to the National Association of Small Business Investment Companies, as of December 2000 there were 404 operating SBICs with over $16 billion under management. Since 1958, the SBIC program has provided approximately $27 billion of long-term debt and equity capital to nearly 90,000 small U.S. companies.

SBICs are limited by law to taking minority shareholder positions and can invest no more than 20 percent of their equity capital in any one situation. Because SBICs borrow much of their capital from the SBA and must service this debt, they prefer to make some form of interest-bearing investment. Four common forms of financing are long-term loans with options to buy stock, convertible debentures, straight loans, and, in some cases, preferred stock. In the year 2002, the average financing by bank SBICs was $4 million. The median for all SBICs was $250,000.[20] Due to their SBA debt, SBICs tend not to finance start-ups and early-stage companies but to make investments in more mature companies. According to the SBA, major changes have been made in the SBIC program over the last few years, including the Small Business Program Improvement Act of 1996, which states in its declaration of policy:

Research and development are major factors in the growth and progress of industry and the national economy. The expense of carrying on research and development programs is beyond the means of many small-business concerns, and such concerns are handicapped in obtaining the benefits of research and development programs conducted at Government expense. These small-business concerns are thereby placed at a competitive disadvantage. This weakens the competitive free enterprise system and prevents the orderly development of the national economy. It is the policy of the Congress that assistance be given to small-business concerns to enable them to undertake and to obtain the benefits of research and development in order to maintain and strengthen the competitive free enterprise system and the national economy.[21]

Mezzanine Capital*

Once your company has overcome many of the early-stage risks, it may be ready for mezzanine capital. The term *mezzanine financing* refers to capital that is between senior debt financing and common stock. In some cases it takes the form of redeemable preferred stock, but in most cases it is subordinated debt that carries an equity "kicker" consisting of warrants or a conversion feature into common stock. This subordinated-debt capital has many characteristics of debt but also can serve as equity to underpin senior debt. It is generally unsecured, with a fixed percentage return and maturity of five to ten years. A number of variables are involved in structuring such a loan: the interest rate, the amount and form of the equity, exercise/conversion price, maturity, call features, sinking fund, covenants, and put/call options. These variables provide for a wide range of possible structures to suit the needs of both the issuer and the investor.

Offsetting these advantages are a few drawbacks to mezzanine capital as compared to equity capital. As debt, the interest is payable on a regular basis, and the principal must be repaid, if not converted into equity. This is a large claim against cash and can be burdensome if the

*This section is drawn from Donald P. Remey, "Mezzanine Financing: A Flexible Source of Growth Capital," in *Pratt's Guide to Venture Capital Sources*, ed. David Schutt (New York: Venture Economics Publishing, 1993), pp. 84–86.

expected growth and/or profitability does not materialize and cash becomes tight. In addition, the subordinated debt often contains covenants relating to net worth, debt, and dividends.

Mezzanine investors generally look for companies that have a demonstrated performance record, with revenues approaching $10 million or more. Since the financing will involve paying interest, the investor will carefully examine existing and future cash flow and projections.

Mezzanine financing is utilized in a wide variety of industries, ranging from basic manufacturing to high technology. As the name implies, however, it focuses more on the broad middle spectrum of business, rather than on high-tech, high-growth companies. Specialty retailing, broadcasting, communications, environmental services, distributors, and consumer or business service industries are more attractive to mezzanine investors.

Private Placements

Private placements are an attractive source of equity capital for a private company that for whatever reason has ruled out the possibility of going public. If the goal of the company is to raise a specific amount of capital in a short period of time, this equity source may be the answer. In this transaction, the company offers stock to a few private investors, rather than to the public as in a public offering. A private placement requires little paperwork compared to a public offering, in addition to the fact that the time period for this private transaction can be shorter.

If your management team knows of enough investors, then the private placement could be distributed among a small group of friends, family, relatives, or acquaintances. Or the company may decide to have a broker circulate the proposal among a few investors who have expressed an interest in small companies.

Initial Public Stock Offerings

Commonly referred to as an IPO, an *initial public offering* raises capital through federally registered and underwritten sales of the company's shares. Numerous federal and state securities laws and regulations govern these offerings; thus, it is important that management consult with lawyers and accountants who are intimately familiar with the current regulations.

In the past, such as during the strong bull market for new issues that occurred in 1983, 1986, 1992, and 1996, it was possible to raise money for an early-growth venture or even for a start-up. These boom markets are easy to identify because the number of new issues jumped from 78 in 1980 to an astounding 523 in 1983, representing a jump from about $1 billion in 1980 to about twelve times that figure in 1983 (see Exhibit 5.9). Another boom came three years later, in 1986, when the number of new issues reached 464. Although 1992's number of new issues (396) did not exceed the 1986 performance, a record $22.2 billion was raised in IPOs. Accounting for this reduction in the number of new issues and the increase in the amounts raised, one observer commented, "the average size of each 1983 deal was a quarter of the $70 million average for the deals done."[22] In other, more difficult financial environments, most dramatically, following the stock market crash on October 19, 1987, the new-issues market became very quiet for entrepreneurial companies, especially compared to the hot market of 1986. As a result, exit opportunities were limited. In addition, it was very difficult to raise money for early-growth or even more mature companies from the public market.

The more mature a company is when it makes a public offering, the better its terms will be. A higher valuation can be placed on the company, and less equity will be given up by the founders for the required capital.

An entrepreneurial company might choose to go public to realize some of the following advantages:

- To raise more capital with less dilution than occurs with private placements or venture capital
- To improve the balance sheet and/or to reduce or to eliminate debt, thereby enhancing the company's net worth
- To obtain cash for pursuing opportunities that would otherwise be unaffordable

Exhibit 5.9 Initial Public Offerings (1980–2003)

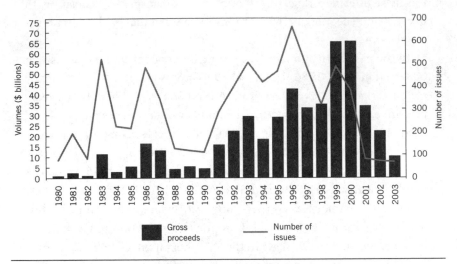

Source: http://bear.cba.ufl.edu/ritter. Table 5 of "Some Factoids About the 2003 IPO Market" under "IPO Data." Jay R. Ritter, University of Florida.

- To access other suppliers of capital and to increase bargaining power, as the company pursues additional capital when it needs it least
- To improve credibility with customers, vendors, key people, and prospects
- To give the impression of "playing in the big leagues"
- To achieve liquidity for owners and investors
- To create options to acquire other companies with a tax-free exchange of stock, rather than having to use cash
- To create equity incentives for new and existing employees

Notwithstanding the above, IPOs can be disadvantageous for a number of reasons:

- The legal, accounting, and administrative costs of raising money via a public offering are more disadvantageous than other ways of raising money.
- A large amount of management effort, time, and expense are required to comply with SEC regulations and reporting

requirements and to maintain the status of a public company. This diversion from the tasks of running the company can adversely affect its performance and growth.

- Management can become more interested in maintaining the price of the company's stock and computing capital gains than in running the company. Short-term activities to maintain or increase a current year's earnings can take precedence over longer-term programs to build the company and increase its earnings.
- The liquidity of a company's stock achieved through a public offering may be more apparent than real. Without a sufficient number of shares outstanding and a strong "market maker," there may be no real market for the stock and, thus, no liquidity.
- The investment banking firms willing to take a new or unseasoned company public may not be the ones with whom the company would like to do business and establish a long-term relationship.

Private Placement After Going Public[23]

Sometimes a company goes public and then, for any number of reasons that add up to bad luck, the high expectations that attracted lots of investors in the first place turn sour. Your financial picture worsens; there is a cash crisis; subsequently the price of your stock goes down in the public marketplace. You find that you need new funds to work your way out of difficulties, but now public investors are disillusioned and not likely to cooperate if you bring out a new issue.

Still, other investors are sophisticated enough to see beyond today's problems; they know the company's fundamentals are sound. Although the public has turned its back on you, these investors may well be receptive if you offer a private placement to tide you over. In such circumstances, you may use a wide variety of securities—common stock, convertible preferred stock, or convertible debentures. There are also several types of exempt offerings. They are usually described by reference to the securities regulation that applies to them.

Regulation D is the result of the first cooperative effort by the SEC and the state securities associations to develop a uniform exemption from registration for small issuers. A significant number of states allow for qualification under state law in coordination with the qualification under Regulation D. Heavily regulated states, such as California, are notable exceptions. However, even in California, the applicable exemption is fairly consistent with the Regulation D concept.

Although Regulation D outlines procedures for exempt offerings, there is a requirement to file certain information (Form D) with the SEC. Form D is a relatively short form that asks for certain general information about the issuer and the securities, as well as some specific data about the expenses of the offering and the intended use of the proceeds.

Regulation D provides exemptions from registration when securities are being sold in certain circumstances. The various circumstances are commonly referred to by the applicable Regulation D rule number. The rules and their application are as follows:

- **Rule 504.** Issuers that are not subject to the reporting obligations of the Securities Exchange Act of 1934 (nonpublic companies) and that are not investment companies may sell up to $1 million worth of securities over a twelve-month period to an unlimited number of investors.
- **Rule 505.** Issuers that are not investment companies may sell up to $5 million worth of securities over a twelve-month period to no more than thirty-five nonaccredited purchasers, and to an unlimited number of accredited investors. Such issuers may be eligible for this exemption even though they are public companies (subject to the reporting requirements of the 1934 act).
- **Rule 506.** Issuers may sell an unlimited number of securities to no more than thirty-five unaccredited but sophisticated purchasers, and to an unlimited number of accredited purchasers. Public companies may be eligible for this exemption.

Employee Stock Option Plans (ESOPs)

ESOPs are another potential source of funding used by existing companies that have high confidence in the stability of their future earnings and cash flow. An ESOP is a program in which the employees become investors in the company, thereby creating an internal source of funding. An ESOP is a tax-qualified retirement benefit plan. In essence, an ESOP borrows money, usually from a bank or insurance company, and uses the cash proceeds to buy the company's stock (usually from the owners or the treasury). The stock then becomes collateral for the bank note, while the owners or treasury have cash that can be used for a variety of purposes. For the lender, 50 percent of the interest earned on the loan to the ESOP is tax exempt. The company makes annual tax-deductible contributions—of both interest and principal—to the ESOP in an amount needed to service the bank loan. "The combination of being able to invest in employer stock and to benefit from its many tax advantages make the ESOP an attractive tool."[24]

Keeping Current About Capital Markets

One picture is vivid from all this: capital markets, especially for closely held, private companies right through the initial public offering, are dynamic, volatile, asymmetrical, and imperfect. Keeping abreast of what is happening in the capital markets in the six to twelve months prior to a major capital infusion can save invaluable time and hundreds of thousands, and occasionally millions, of dollars. Some of the best sources currently available to keep you informed include the following:

- National Venture Capital Association (nvca.org)
- Daniel R. Garner, Robert R. Owen, and Robert R. Conway, *The Ernst & Young Guide to Raising Capital* (New York: John Wiley & Sons, 1991)
- David Schutt, ed., *Pratt's Guide to Venture Capital Sources* (New York: Venture Economics Publishing, 2003)
- *Venture Capital Journal* (published monthly by Venture Economics Publishing)
- *Venture Finance* (IPO Reporter)
- *Inc.*
- *Red Herring* (a Silicon Valley magazine)
- *Venture One* (database and reports on venture capital from California)

Conclusion

Appreciating the capital markets as a food chain looking for companies to invest in is key to understanding their motivations and requirements. You have to determine the need and desire for outside investors and who they should be.

America's unique capital markets include a wide array of private investors, from angels to venture capitalists. The search for capital can be very time consuming, and whom you obtain money from is often more important than how much.

It is said that the only thing that is harder to get from a venture capitalist than a "yes" is a "no." Fortunately for you, the booming rebirth of classic venture capital in the 1990s has raised the valuations and the sources available. Those small business owners who know what and whom to look for—and look out for—increase their odds for success.

Notes

1. Taken from a lecture on March 4, 1993, at the Harvard Business School, given by Paul A. Maeder and Robert F. Higgins of Highland Capital Partners, a Boston venture capital firm.

2. Robert A. Mamis, "The Secrets of Bootstrapping," *Inc.*, Sept. 1992, p. 72.

3. Ibid., p. 76.

4. G. Baty, "Initial Financing of the New Research Based Enterprise in New England," Federal Reserve Bank of Boston Research Report No. 25 (Boston, MA, 1964); and G. Baty, "Entrepreneurship: Play to Win" (Reston, VA: Reston Publishing, 1974), p. 97.

5. SEC Regulation D, Rules 504–506.

6. Mark Van Osnabrugge and Robert J. Robinson, *Angel Investing: Matching Startup Funds with Startup Companies—A Guide for Entrepreneurs, Individual Investors, and Venture Capitalists* (San Francisco: Jossey-Bass, May 2000).

7. William H. Wetzel Jr., "Informal Investors—When and Where to Look," in *Pratt's Guide to Venture Capital Sources*, 6th ed., ed. Stanley E. Pratt (Wellesley Hills, MA: Capital Publishing, 1982), p. 22.

8. Ibid.

9. "Note on the Venture Capital Industry (1981)," HBS Case 285-096 (Harvard Business School, 1982), p. 1.

10. Michael Vachon, "Venture Capital Reborn," *Venture Capital Journal*, Jan. 1993, p. 32.

11. Ibid.

12. *Venture Economics National Venture Capital Association Yearbook* (2003).

13. Bygrave and Timmons, *Venture Capital at the Crossroads*, p. 11.

14. For more specifics, see Harry A. Sapienza and Jeffry A. Timmons, "Launching and Building Entrepreneurial Companies: Do the Venture Capitalists Build Value?" in Proceedings of the Babson Entrepreneurship Research Conference, May 1989, Babson Park, MA. See also Jeffry A. Timmons, "Venture Capital: More than Money," in *Pratt's Guide to Venture Capital Sources*, 13th ed., ed. Jane Morris (Needham, MA: Venture Economics, 1989), p. 71.

15. Geoffrey H. Smart, "Management Assessment Methods in Venture Capital," unpublished doctoral dissertation (Claremont Graduate University, 1998), p. 109.

16. This data was compiled from the Small Business Administration, sba.gov.

17. Daniel R. Garner, Robert R. Owen, and Robert P. Conway, *The Ernst & Young Guide to Raising Capital* (New York: John Wiley & Sons, 1991), pp. 165–66.

18. The National Association of Small Business Investment Companies (NASBIC), nasbic.org.

19. Small Business Administration, sba.gov.

20. NASBIC, nasbic.org.

21. *U.S. Code*, title 15, chapter 14A, sec. 638.

22. Thomas N. Cochran, "IPOs Everywhere: New Issues Hit a Record in the First Quarter," *Barron's*, April 19, 1993, p. 14.

23. Garner, Owen, and Conway, *The Ernst & Young Guide to Raising Capital*, pp. 52–54.

24. Ibid.

CHAPTER 6

THE DEAL
VALUATION, STRUCTURE, AND NEGOTIATION

"Always assume the deal will not close, and keep several alternatives alive."

—JAMES HINDMAN, FOUNDER, CHIEF EXECUTIVE OFFICER, AND CHAIR, JIFFY LUBE INTERNATIONAL

The Art and Craft of Valuation

The small business owner's and private investor's world of finance is very different from the corporate finance arena, where public companies jostle and compete in well-established capital markets. The private company and private capital world of entrepreneurial finance is more volatile and imperfect and less accessible. The sources of capital are very different. The companies are usually younger and more dynamic, and the environment more rapidly changing and uncertain. The consequences, for entrepreneurs and investors alike, of this markedly different context are profound. First, cash is king and beta coefficients and elegant corporate financial theories are irrelevant. Liquidity and timing are everything, and there are innumerable, unavoidable conflicts between users and suppliers of capital. Finally, the determination of a company's value is quite elusive, and more art than science.

What Is a Company Worth?

The answer: it all depends! Unlike the market for public companies, where millions of shares are traded daily and the firm's market capitalization (total shares outstanding times the price per share) is readily determined, the market for private companies is very imperfect.

Determinants of Value

The message here is simple. The criteria and methods applied in corporate finance to value companies traded publicly in the capital markets, when cavalierly applied to entrepreneurial companies, have severe limitations. The ingredients of the entrepreneurial valuation are cash, time, and risk.

Long-Term Value Creation Versus Quarterly Earnings

The core mission of the entrepreneur is to build the best company possible and, if possible, a great company. This is the single surest way of generating long-term value for all the stakeholders and society. Such a mission has quite different strategic imperatives than one aimed solely at maximizing quarterly earnings in order to attain the highest share price possible given price/earnings ratios at the time. (More will be said about this in the last chapter of the book.)

Psychological Factors Determining Value

Time after time companies are valued at preposterous multiples of any sane price/earnings (P/E) or sales ratios. In the best years—for example, the 1982–1983 bull market—the New York Stock Exchange Index was trading at nearly twenty times earnings; it sank to around eight after the stock market crash of October 1987. Even twelve to fifteen times earnings would be considered good in many years. By 1998 to late 2001, the S&P 500 was setting above a P/E of thirty. A late 1990s survey of the top one hundred public companies in Massachusetts showed these stocks were being traded at fifty or more times earnings; several were at ninety-five to one hundred times earnings and six to seven times *sales!* Even more extreme valuations were seen during the peak of the so-called dot-com bubble from 1998 to early 2000. Some companies were valued at one hundred times revenue and more during this classic frenzy, echoing the tulip mania of centuries past. Most of the dot-coms that survived the dot-"bomb" phase lost 90 percent of their value!

Often what is behind extraordinarily high valuations is a psychological wave, a combination of euphoric enthusiasm for a fine company, exacerbated by greed and fear—of missing the run-up. The same psychology can also drive prices to undreamed-of heights in private companies. In the late 1960s, for instance, Xerox bought Scientific Data Systems, then at $100 million in sales and earning $10 million after taxes, for $1 billion: ten times sales and one hundred times earnings! The pattern of big companies paying huge sums for small firms continually repeats. Between 1997 and 2000, telecom firms like Nortel and Lucent bought small firms that had minimal if any revenue, earning small business founders hundreds of millions. Value is also in the eye of the beholder.

A Broad Look at Valuation

Establishing Boundaries and Ranges, Rather than Calculating a Number. Valuation is much more than science, as can be seen from the examples just noted. As will be seen shortly, there are at least a dozen different ways of determining the value of a private company. A lot of assumptions and a lot of judgment calls are made in every valuation exercise. It can be a serious mistake, therefore, to approach the valuation task in hopes of arriving at a single number or even a quite narrow range. All you can realistically expect is a range of values with boundaries driven by different methods and underlying assumptions. Within that range the buyer and the seller need to determine the comfort zone of each. At what point are you basically indifferent to buying and selling? Determining your point of indifference can be an invaluable aid in preparing you for negotiations to buy or sell.

Valuation is an important exercise for the growth-minded small business owner who is seeking capital. For you to make a deal to acquire an investment, the investor is likely to want a share of the company (in one form or another). We will discuss a number of valuation methods but first consider how and why you might want to make a deal.

What Is a Deal?[1]

Deals are defined as economic agreements between at least two parties. In the context of entrepreneurial finance, most deals involve the allocation of cash-flow streams (with respect to both amount and timing), the allocation of risk, and hence the allocation of value between different groups. For example, deals can be made between suppliers and users of capital, or between management and employees of a venture.

A Way of Thinking About Deals over Time. To assess and to design long-lived deals, Professor William A. Sahlman from Harvard Business School suggests the following series of questions as a guide for deal makers in structuring and in understanding how deals evolve over time:[2]

- Who are the players?
- What are their goals and objectives?
- What risks do they perceive and how have these risks been managed?
- What problems do they perceive?
- How much do they have invested, both in absolute terms and relative terms, at cost and at market value?
- What is the context surrounding the current decision?
- What is the form of their current investment or claim on the company?
- What power do they have to act? To precipitate change?
- What real options do they have? How long does it take them to act?

- What credible threats do they have?
- How and from whom do they get information?
- How credible is the source of information?
- What will be the value of their claim under different scenarios?
- How can they get value for their claims?
- To what degree can they appropriate value from another party?
- How much uncertainty characterizes the situation?
- What are the rules of the game (e.g., tax, legislative)?
- What is the context (e.g., state of economy, capital markets, industry specifics) at the current time? How is the context expected to change?

Investor's Required Rate of Return (IRR)

One of the first things you have to do when seeking investment is to understand the return requirements of the investor. Various investors will require a different rate of return (ROR) for investments in different stages of development and will expect holding periods of various lengths. For example, Exhibit 6.1 summarizes, as ranges, the annual RORs that venture capital investors seek on investments in firms by stage of development and how long they expect to hold these investments. Several factors underlie the required ROR on a venture capital

Exhibit 6.1 Rate of Return by Venture Capital Investors

Stage	Annual ROR (%)	Typical Expected Holding Period (years)
Seed and start-up	50–100% or more	More than 10 years
First stage	40–60	5–10
Second stage	30–40	4–7
Expansion*	20–30	3–5
Bridge and mezzanine	20–30	1–3
LBOs	30–50	3–5
Turnarounds	50+	3–5

*Expansion, bridge, and mezzanine rounds are likely areas of need for the small existing firm seeking to grow.

investment, including premium for systemic risk,* a lack of liquidity, and value added. Of course, these can be expected to vary regionally and from time to time as market conditions change, because the investments are in what are decidedly imperfect capital-market niches to begin with.

Valuation Methods

The Venture Capital Method

This method is appropriate for investments in a company with negative cash flows at the time of the investment, but that in a number of years is projected to generate significant earnings. The steps involved in this method are as follows:

1. Estimate the company's *net income* in a number of years, at which time the investor plans on harvesting. This estimate will be based on sales and margin projections presented by the entrepreneur in his or her business plan.
2. Determine the appropriate *price-to-earning ratio*, or P/E ratio. The appropriate P/E ratio can be determined by studying current multiples for companies with similar economic characteristics.
3. Calculate the projected *terminal value* by multiplying the expected net income at the point you expect to provide liquidity to your investors times the P/E ratio.
4. The terminal value can then be discounted to find the *present value* of the investment. Venture capitalists use discount rates ranging from 35 percent to 80 percent (these discount rates coincide with the expected RORs listed in Exhibit 6.1), because of the risk involved in these types of investments.
5. To determine the investor's *required percentage of ownership*, based on the initial investment, the initial investment is divided by the estimated present value.

*Systemic risk involves the variables in the economic environment that you simply can't control, such as a war, a disease outbreak like SARS, or even a political quandary like the 2000 presidential election. Uncertain outcomes of events create risk.

To summarize the above steps, the following formula can be used:

$$\text{Final ownership required} = \frac{\text{Required future value (investment)}}{\text{Total terminal value}}$$

$$= \frac{(1 + IRR)^{years} \text{ (investment)}}{\text{P/E ratio (terminal net income)}}$$

Finally, the number of shares and the share price must be calculated by using the following formula:

$$\text{New shares} = \frac{\text{Percentage of ownership required by the investor}}{1 - \text{Percentage of ownership required by investor}} \times \text{old shares}$$

By definition, the share price equals the price paid divided by the number of shares.

This method is commonly used by venture capitalists, because they make equity investments in industries often requiring a large initial investment with significant projected revenues, in addition to the fact that in the negotiations, the percentage of ownership is a key issue.

The growth-minded small business can affect the variables in the calculation to their advantage. Because you have a proven market and a positive cash flow, the rate of return required by the investor is lowered from the start-up 40–70 percent to a growth company 25–40 percent return. This will effectively reduce the amount of equity you'll have to surrender for investment by as much as one-half!

The Fundamental Method

The fundamental method is simply the present value of the future earnings stream (see Exhibit 6.2). The fundamental method can be problematic for you because earnings, in a growth company, are pushed into the future. Once a company decides on a high-potential growth strategy, there are no calculable earnings because all cash (and earnings) is applied to increasing the growth rate. The purpose of this strategy is to reap a huge increase in earnings in future years. But remember, the

Exhibit 6.2 Example of the Fundamental Method for Hitech, Inc.

Year	Percentage Growth of Revenue	Revenue (Millions)	After-Tax Margin	After-Tax Profit	Present Value Factor	Present Value of Each Year's Earnings
1	50%	$3.00	-0-	-0-	1.400	-0-
2	50	4.50	4.0%	$0.18	1.960	$0.09
3	50	6.75	7.0	0.47	2.744	0.17
4	50	10.13	9.0	0.91	3.842	0.24
5	50	15.19	11.0	1.67	5.378	0.31
6	40	21.26	11.5	2.45	7.530	0.33
7	30	27.64	12.0	3.32	10.541	0.32
8	20	33.17	12.0	3.98	14.758	0.27
9	15	38.15	12.0	4.58	20.661	0.22
10	10	41.96	12.0	5.03	28.926	0.17
Total present value of earnings in the super growth period						2.12
Residual future value of earnings stream				$63.00	28.926	2.18
Total present value of company						4.30

investors' required rate of return is annualized. So each year the pay-back to the investor is delayed, the amount of money required to satisfy the investor is greatly increased.

The First Chicago Method[3]

Another alternative valuation method, developed at First Chicago Corporation's venture capital group, employs a lower discount rate, but applies it to an *expected* cash flow. That expected cash flow is the average of three possible scenarios, with each scenario weighted according to its perceived probability. The equation to determine the investor's required final ownership is:

$$\text{Required final ownership} = \frac{\text{Future value of investment} - \text{Future value of non-IPO cash flow}}{\text{Probability (success)} \times \text{(Forecast terminal value)}}$$

This formula differs from the original basic venture capital formula in two ways.[4] First, the basic formula assumes that there are no cash flows between the investment and the harvest in year 5. The future value of the immediate cash flows is subtracted from the future value of the investment because the difference between them is what must be made up for out of the terminal value. Second, the basic formula does not distinguish between the *forecast* terminal value and the *expected* terminal value. The traditional method uses the forecast terminal value, which is adjusted through the use of a high discount rate. The formula employs the expected value of the terminal value. Exhibit 6.3 shows an example of this method.

Ownership Dilution[5]

In addition to estimating the appropriate discount rate for the current round, the first-round venture capitalist must now estimate the discount rates that are most likely to be applied in the following rounds, which are projected for years 2 and 4. Although a 50 percent rate is still appro-

Exhibit 6.3 Example of the First Chicago Method

	Success	Sideways Survival	Failure
1. Revenue growth rate (from base of $2 million)	60%	15%	0%
2. Revenue after 3 years	$8.19 million	$3.04 million (liquidation)	$2 million
3. Revenue after 5 years	$20.97 million (IPO)	$4.02 million	
4. Revenue level after 7 years		$5.32 million (acquisition)	
5. After-tax profit margin and earnings at liquidity	15%: $3.15 million	7%: $0.37 million	
6. Price-earnings ratio at liquidity	17	7	
7. Value of company liquidity	$53.55 million	$2.61 million	$0.69 million
8. Present value of company using discount rate of 40%	$9.96 million	$0.25 million	$0.25 million
9. Probability of each scenario	.4	.4	.2
10. Expected present value of the company under each scenario	$3.98 million	$0.10 million	$0.05 million
11. Expected present value of the company		$4.13 million	
12. Percentage ownership required to invest $2.5 million		60.5%	

priate for year 0, it is estimated that investors in Hitech, Inc., will demand a 40 percent return in year 2 and a 25 percent return in year 4. The final ownership that each investor must be left with, given a terminal price/earnings ratio of 15, can be calculated using the basic valuation formula:

Round 1:

$$\text{Final \%} = \frac{\text{Future value (investment)}}{\text{Terminal value (company)}} = \frac{1.50^5 \times \$1.5 \text{ million}}{15. \times \$2.5 \text{ million}} = 30.4\% \text{ ownership}$$

Round 2:

$$(1.40^3 \times \$1 \text{ million}) / (15 \times \$2.5 \text{ million}) = 7.3\%$$

Round 3:

$$(1.25^1 \times \$1 \text{ million}) / (15 \times \$1.5 \text{ million}) = 3.3\%$$

Discounted Cash Flow

In a simple discounted cash-flow method, three time periods are defined: (1) years 1–5; (2) years 6–10; and (3) years 11–infinity. The necessary operating assumptions for each period are initial sales, growth rates, EBIAT/sales, and (net fixed assets + operating working capital)/sales. While using this method, one should also note relationships and trade-offs. With these assumptions, the discount rate can be applied to the weighted average cost of capital (WACC).* Then the value for free cash flow (years 1–10) is added to the terminal value. This terminal value is the growth perpetuity.

Other Rule-of-Thumb Valuation Methods

Several other valuation methods are also employed to estimate the value of a company. Many of these are based on the most recent transactions of similar firms, established by a sale of the company or a prior investment. Such comparables may look at several different multiples, such as

---

*Note that it is WACC, not free cash flow, because of the tax factor.

earnings, free cash flow, revenue, EBIT, and book value. Knowledge-able investment bankers and venture capitalists make it their business to know the activity on the current market place for private capital and how deals are being priced. These methods are used most often to value an existing company, rather than a start-up, since there are so many more knowns about the company and its financial performance. The rate of return required by the investor determines the investor's required share of the ownership.

As a final note, one can readily see that if any key variable—the amount of investment, profit, required return, or industry price/earn-ings ratio—is changed, the percentage of ownership will change also.

If the venture capitalists require the RORs mentioned earlier, the ownership they also require is determined as follows: in the start-up stage, 25–75 percent for investing all of the required funds; beyond the start-up stage, 10–40 percent, depending on the amount invested, matu-rity, and track record of the venture; in a seasoned venture in the later rounds of investment, 10–30 percent to supply the additional funds needed to sustain its growth. Exhibit 6.4 reflects the relative return an investor will expect at each stage of a company's life.

Exhibit 6.4 Investor's Required Share Ownership Under Various ROR Objectives

Assumptions:
Amount of initial startup investment = $1 million   Year 5 after-tax profit = $1 million
Holding period = 5 years   Year 5 price/earnings ratio = 15
Required rate of return = 50%
Calculating the required share of ownership:

Price/Earning Ratio	Investor's Return Objective (Percent/Year Compounded)			
	30%	40%	50%	60%
10×	37	54	76	106
15×	25	36	51	70
20×	19	27	38	52
25×	15	22	30	42

The Reality

The past two and a half decades have seen the venture capital industry explode from investing only $50–$100 million per year to nearly $100 *billion* in 2000. Exhibit 6.5 shows how the many realities of the marketplace for capital are at work, and how current market conditions, deal flow, and relative bargaining power influence the actual deal struck. The dot-bomb explosion and the plummeting of the capital markets led to much lower values for private companies. The NASDAQ index fell from over 5000 to less than 1200, a 76 percent decline.

The Down Round or Cram Down Circa 2002

In this environment, which also existed after the October 1987 stock-market crash, entrepreneurs face rude shocks in the second or third round of financing. Instead of a substantial four or even five times

Exhibit 6.5 The Reality

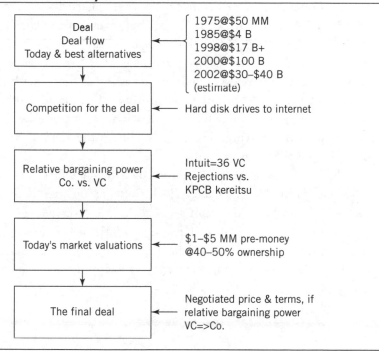

increase in the valuation from series A to B, or B to C, they are jolted with what is called a "cram down" round: the price is typically one-fourth to two-thirds of the last round. This severely dilutes the founders' ownership, as investors are normally protected against dilution. Founder dilution from a failure to perform is one thing, but dilution because the NASDAQ and IPO markets collapsed seems rudely unfair. But that is part of the reality of valuation.

In many financings in 2001, and into 2002, onerous additional conditions were imposed, such as a three to five times return to the series C investors *before* series A or B investors receive a single dime! One can readily see that both the founders and early-round investors are severely punished by such cram-down financings. The principle of *the last money in governing the deal* terms still prevails.

One can sense just how vulnerable and volatile the valuation of a company can be in these imperfect markets when external events, such as the collapse of NASDAQ, trigger a downward spiral. One also gains a new perspective on how critically important timing is. Many strongly performing companies were crammed down. Imagine those companies that didn't meet their plans: they were pummeled, if financed at all. What a startling reversal from the dot-com boom in 1998–1999, when companies at *concept stage* (with no products, no identifiable or defensible models of how they would make money or even break even, and no management teams with proven experience) raised $20 million, $50 million, $70 million, and more, *and* had IPOs with multibillion valuations. History asks: what is wrong with this picture? History also offers the answer: happiness is still a positive cash flow!

Thereafter most investors retreated to the sidelines and stopped investing. From 2000 into early 2003, funds rationalized their investments with dramatic downward revaluations and reserved huge quantities of cash. Then in the second quarter of 2003, venture money started going into existing, growth-oriented firms. Indeed, more than half of the biggest venture investments went to growth in the second quarter of that year.[6]

Inherent Conflicts Between Users and Suppliers of Capital[7]

There are several inherent conflicts between you, the users of capital, and investors, the suppliers of capital. Whereas you want to have as much time as possible for the financing, the investors want to supply capital just in time or to invest only when the company needs the money. You should be thinking of raising money when you do not need it, while preserving the option to find another source of capital.

Similarly, you will want to raise as much money as possible, while the investors want to supply just enough capital in staged capital commitments. The investors, such as venture capitalists, use staged capital commitments to manage their risk exposure over six- to twelve-month increments of investing.

In the negotiations of a deal, you might become attracted to a high valuation with the sentiment "My price, your terms." The investors will thus focus on a low valuation, asserting, "My price *and* my terms."

This tension applies not only to financial transactions but also to the styles of the users versus the styles of the suppliers of capital. The users value their independence and treasure the flexibility their company has brought them. However, the investors are hoping to preserve their options as well. These options usually include both reinvesting and abandoning the venture.

These points of view also clash in the composition of the board of directors, where the entrepreneur seeks control and independence, and the investors want the right to control the board if the company does not perform as well as was expected. This sense of control is an emotional issue for most entrepreneurs, who want to be in charge of their own destiny. Prizing their autonomy and self-determination, many of these users of capital would agree with the passion Walt Disney conveyed in the following statement:

I've always been bored with just making money. I've wanted to do things different ways. Some of them say, "This guy has no regard for money." That is not true. I have regard for money. But I'm not like

> *some people who worship money as something you've got to have piled*
> *up in a big pile somewhere. I've only thought of money in one way, and*
> *that is to do something with it, you see? I don't think there is a thing*
> *that I own that I will ever get the benefit of, except through doing*
> *things with it.*[8]

The investors may believe in your passion, but they still want to protect themselves with first refusals, initial public offering rights, and various other exit options.

Your long-term goals and those of the suppliers of capital may also
be contradictory. You may be content with the progress of your venture and happy with a single or double. Yet the investors will not be
quite as content with moderate success, but instead want their capital to
produce extraordinary returns—they want a home run from you. Thus,
the pressures put on you may seem unwarranted, yet necessary for the
investor.

These strategies contradict each other when they are manifested in
the management styles of the users and providers of capital. When you
are willing to take a calculated risk or are working to minimize and
avoid unnecessary risks, the investor has bet on the art of the exceptional and thus is willing to gamble the farm every day.

Finally, the ultimate goals may differ. The entrepreneur who continues to build his or her company may find operating a company enjoy-
able. The definition of success both personally and for the company may
involve long-term company building, such that a sustainable institution
is created. But the investors will want to cash out in two to five years,
so that they can reinvest their capital in another venture.

Tools for Managing Risk/Reward

In a deal, the claims on cash and equity are prioritized by the players.
Some of the tools available to the players are common stock, partnerships, preferred stock (dividend and liquidation preference), debt
(secured, unsecured, personally guaranteed, or convertible), performance conditional pricing (ratchets or positive incentives), puts and

calls, warrants, and cash. Some of the critical aspects of a deal go beyond just the money:

- Number, type, and mix of stocks (and perhaps of stock and debt) and various features that may go with them (such as puts) that affect the investor's rate of return
- The amounts and timing of takedowns, conversions, and the like
- Interest rates on debt or preferred shares
- The number of seats, and who actually will represent investors, on the board of directors
- Possible changes in the management team and in the composition of the board
- Registration rights for investors' stock (in the case of a registered public offering)
- Right of first refusal granted to the investor on subsequent private placements or an IPO
- Employment, noncompete, and proprietary rights agreements
- The payment of legal, accounting, consulting, or other fees connected with putting the deal together
- Specific performance targets for revenues, expenses, market penetration, and so on, by certain target dates

These are some of the questions that may help in identifying the bets of the players:

- What is the bet?
- Who is it for?
- Who is taking the risk? Who receives the rewards?
- Who should be making these bets?
- What will happen if the entrepreneurs exceed the venture capitalists' expectations? If they fall short?
- What are the incentives for the money managers? Consequences of their success or failure to perform?
- How will the money managers behave? What will be their investing strategy?

Some of the Lessons Learned

The following tips may help to minimize many of these surprises:

- Raise money when you do not need it.
- Learn as much about the process and how to manage it as you can.
- Know your relative bargaining position.
- If all you get is money, you are not getting much.
- Assume the deal will never close.
- Always have a backup source of capital.
- The legal and other experts can blow it—sweat the details yourself!
- Users of capital are invariably at a disadvantage in dealing with the suppliers of capital.
- If you are out of cash when you seek to raise capital, suppliers of capital will eat your lunch.

Negotiations

Negotiations have been defined by many experts in a variety of ways, as the following examples demonstrate. Herb Cohen, the author of *You Can Negotiate Anything*, defines negotiations as "a field of knowledge and endeavor that focuses on gaining the favor of people from whom we want things,"[9] or, similarly, as "the use of information and power to affect behavior within a 'web of tension.'"[10] Other experts in the field of negotiations, Roger Fisher and William Ury, assert that negotiations are a "back-and-forth communication designed to reach an agreement when you and the other side have some interests that are shared and others that are opposed."[11]

What Is Negotiable?

Far more is negotiable than entrepreneurs think.[12] For instance, a normal ploy of the attorney representing the investors is to insist, matter-of-factly, that "this is our boilerplate" and that the entrepreneur should take it or leave it. Yet, it is possible for an entrepreneur to negotiate and craft an agreement that represents his or her needs.

During the negotiation, the investors will be evaluating the negotiating skills, intelligence, and maturity of the entrepreneur. The entrepreneur has precisely the same opportunity to size up the investor. If the investors see anything that shakes their confidence or trust, they probably will withdraw from the deal. Similarly, if an investor turns out to be arrogant, hot-tempered, unwilling to see the other side's needs and to compromise, and seems bent on getting every last ounce out of the deal by locking an entrepreneur into as many of the "burdensome clauses" as is possible, the entrepreneur might well want to withdraw.

Throughout the negotiations, entrepreneurs need to bear in mind that a successful negotiation is one in which both sides believe that they have made a fair deal. The best deals are those in which neither party wins and neither loses, and such deals are possible to negotiate. This approach is further articulated in the works of Roger Fisher and William Ury, who have focused on neither soft nor hard negotiation tactics, but rather on principled negotiation, a method developed at the Harvard Negotiation Project. This method asserts that the purpose of negotiations is "to decide issues on their merits rather than through a haggling process focused on what each side says it will and won't do. It suggests that you look for mutual gains wherever possible, and that where your interests conflict, you should insist that the result be based on some fair standards independent of the will of either side."[13] They continue to describe principled negotiations in the following four points:

People: Separate the people from the problem.
Interests: Focus on interests, not positions.
Options: Generate various possibilities before deciding what to do.
Criteria: Insist that the result be based on some objective standard.

Others have spoken of this method of principled negotiation— for example, Bob Woolf of Bob Woolf Associates, a Boston-based firm that has represented everyone from Larry Bird to Gene Shalit, states simply, "you want the other side to be reasonable, not defensive—to work *with* you. You'll have a better chance of getting what you want. Treat someone the way that you would like to be treated, and you'll be successful most of the time."[14]

The Specific Issues Entrepreneurs Typically Face[15]

You may find some subtle but highly significant issues negotiated. Much attention needs to be paid to the details. Some examples:

- **Cosale provision.** This is a provision by which investors can tender their shares of their stock before an initial public offering. It protects the first-round investors but can cause conflicts with investors in later rounds and can inhibit an entrepreneur's ability to cash out.
- **Ratchet antidilution protection.** This enables the lead investors to get free additional common stock if subsequent shares are ever sold at a price lower than originally paid. This protection can create a "dog-in-the-manger syndrome," whereby first-round investors can prevent the company from raising additional necessary funds during a period of adversity for the company. While nice from the investor's perspective, it ignores the reality that in distress situations, the last money calls the shots on price and deal structure.
- **Washout financing.** This is a strategy of last resort, which wipes out all previously issued stock when existing preferred shareholders will not commit additional funds, thus diluting everyone.
- **Forced buyout.** Under this provision, if management does not find a buyer or cannot take the company public by a certain date, then the investors can proceed to find a buyer at terms they agree upon.
- **Demand registration rights.** Here, investors can demand at least one IPO in three to five years. In reality, such clauses are hard to invoke since the market for new public stock issues, rather than the terms of an agreement, ultimately governs the timing of such events.
- **Piggyback registration rights.** These grant to the investors (and to the entrepreneur, if he or she insists) rights to sell stock at the IPO. Since the underwriters usually make this decision, the clause normally is not enforceable.

- **Key-person insurance.** This requires the company to obtain life insurance on key people. The named beneficiary of the insurance can be either the company or the preferred shareholders.

Sand Traps

Strategic Circumference

Each fund-raising strategy sets in motion some actions and commitments by management that will eventually *scribe a strategic circumference* around the company in terms of its current and future financing choices. These future choices will permit varying degrees of freedom as a result of the previous actions. Those who fail to think through the consequences of a fund-raising strategy and the effect on their degrees of freedom fall into this trap.

It is impossible to avoid strategic circumference completely. And while in some cases scribing a strategic circumference is clearly intentional, others may be unintended and, unfortunately, unexpected. For example, a company that plans to remain private or plans to maintain a 1.5 to 1.0 debt-to-equity ratio has intentionally created a strategic circumference.

Legal Circumference

Many people have an aversion to becoming involved in legal or accounting minutiae. They believe that since they pay sizeable professional fees, their advisors should and will pay attention to the details.

Legal documentation spells out the terms, conditions, responsibilities, and rights of the parties to a transaction. Since different sources have different ways of structuring deals, and since these legal and contractual details come at the *end* of the fund-raising process, an entrepreneur may arrive at a point of no return, facing some very onerous conditions and covenants that are not only very difficult to live with, but also create tight limitations and constraints—legal circumference—on future choices that are potentially disastrous. Entrepreneurs cannot rely on attorneys and advisors to protect them in this vital matter.

To avoid this trap, entrepreneurs need to have a fundamental pre-cept: "The devil is in the details." It is imprudent for an entrepreneur *not* to carefully read final documents and very risky to use a lawyer who is *not* experienced and competent. It also is helpful to keep a few options alive and to conserve cash. This also can keep the other side of the table more conciliatory and flexible.

Attraction to Status and Size

It seems there is a cultural attraction to higher status and larger size, even when it comes to raising capital. Simply targeting the largest or the best-known or most-prestigious firms is a trap entrepreneurs often fall into. These firms are often most visible because of their size and investing activity and because they have been around a long time. Yet because the venture capital industry has become more heterogeneous, as well as for other reasons, such firms may not be a good fit.

It is best to avoid this trap by focusing your efforts toward financial backers, whether debt or equity, who have intimate knowledge and first-hand experience with the technology, marketplace, and networks of expertise in the competitive arena. Focus on those firms with relevant know-how that would characterize a good match.

Unknown Territory

Venturing into unknown territory is another problem. Entrepreneurs need to know the terrain in sufficient detail, particularly the require-ments and alternatives of various equity sources. If they do not, they may make critical strategic blunders and waste time.

An illustration of a fund-raising strategy that was ill conceived and, effectively, a lottery—rather than a well-thought-out and focused search—is a company in the fiber optics industry called Opti-Com.* Opti-Com was a spin-off as a start-up from a well-known public com-pany in the industry. The management team was entirely credible but members were not considered superstars. The business plan suggested the company could achieve the magical $50 million in sales in five

*This is a fictional name for an actual company.

years, which the entrepreneurs were told by an outside advisor was the minimum size that venture capital investors would consider. The plan proposed to raise $750,000 for about 10 percent of the common stock of the company. Realistically, since the firm was a custom supplier for special applications, rather than a provider of a new technology with a significant proprietary advantage, a sales estimate of $10 million to $15 million in five years would have been more plausible. The same advisor urged that their business plan be submitted to sixteen blue-ribbon mainstream venture capital firms in the Boston area. Four months later they had received sixteen rejections. The entrepreneurs then were told to "go see the same quality of venture capital firms in New York." A year later, the founders were nearly out of money and had been unsuccessful in their search for capital. When redirected away from mainstream venture capitalists to a more suitable source, a small fund specifically created in Massachusetts—to provide risk capital for emerging firms that might not be robust enough to attract conventional venture capital but would be a welcome addition to the economic renewal of the state—the fit was right. Opti-Com raised the necessary capital, but at a valuation much more in line with the market for start-up deals.

Opportunity Cost

The lure of money often leads to a most common pitfall—the opportunity cost trap. After all, an entrepreneur's optimism persuades him or her that with good people and products (or services), there has to be a lot of money out there with "our name on it." In the process, entrepreneurs tend to grossly underestimate the real costs of getting the cash in the bank. Further, entrepreneurs also misjudge the time, effort, and creative energy required. Indeed, the degree of effort fund-raising requires is perhaps the least appreciated aspect in obtaining capital. In both these cases, there are opportunity costs in expending these resources in a particular direction when the clock is ticking and the calendar pages are turning.

There are opportunity costs, too, in existing emerging companies. In terms of human capital, it is common for top management to devote as much as half its time trying to raise a major amount of outside capital. Again, this requires a tremendous amount of emotional and physical energy as well, of which there is a finite amount to devote to the daily operating demands of the enterprise. The effect on near-term performance is invariably negative. In addition, if expectations of a successful fund-raising effort are followed by a failure to raise the money, morale can deteriorate and key people can be lost.

Significant opportunity costs are also incurred in forgone business and market opportunities that could have been pursued.

Underestimation of Other Costs

Entrepreneurs tend to underestimate the out-of-pocket costs associated with both raising the money and living with it. Consider the incremental costs a firm must pay after it becomes a public company. The Securities and Exchange Commission requires regular audited financial statements and various reports, there are outside directors' fees and liability insurance premiums, legal fees are associated with more extensive reporting requirements, and so on. These can add up quickly, often to $100,000 or more annually.

Another "cost" that can be easily overlooked is of the disclosure that may be necessary to convince a financial backer to part with his or her money. An entrepreneur may have to reveal much more about the company and his other personal finances than he or she ever imagined. Thus, company weaknesses, ownership and compensation arrangements, personal and corporate financial statements, marketing plans and competitive strategies, and so forth may need to be revealed to people whom the entrepreneur does not really know and trust, and with whom he or she may eventually not do business. In addition, the ability to control access to that information is lost.

Greed

The entrepreneur—especially one who is out of cash, or nearly so— may find *any* investment money irresistible. One of the most exhilarating experiences for an entrepreneur is the prospect of raising that first major slug of outside capital, or obtaining that substantial bank line needed for expansion. But desperation may lead to taking the wrong kind of investment from the wrong kind of investor. If the fundamentals of the company are sound, however, then there is money out there, and it always pays to find the right source.

Being Too Anxious

Usually, after months of hard work finding the right source and negotiating the deal, another trap awaits the hungry but unwary entrepreneur, and all too often the temptation is overwhelming. In this pitfall, entrepreneurs want to believe the deal is done with a handshake (or perhaps with an accompanying letter of intent or an executed term sheet), and they terminate discussions with others prematurely.

Take-the-Money-and-Run Myopia

A final snare in raising money for a company is a take-the-money-and-run myopia that invariably prevents an entrepreneur from evaluating one of the most critical longer-term issues—to what extent can the investor add value to the company beyond the money? It is a rash entrepreneur who takes the money even though he or she is unsure whether the prospective financial partner has the relevant experience and know-how in the market and industry area, the contacts the entrepreneur needs but currently lacks, or the savvy and the reputation that adds value in the relationship with the investor.

As has been said before, the successful growth of a company can be critically impacted by the interaction of the management team and the financial partners. If an effective relationship can be established, the value-added synergy can be a powerful stimulant for success. Many founders overlook the high value-added contributions that some investors are accustomed to making and erroneously opt for a "better deal."

Conclusion

Understanding how the capital markets determine valuation is the key aspect of raising money to grow your venture. When calculating the value of a firm, suppliers of capital must determine the probability that a company will achieve the growth goals to which they aspire. That is the heart of the risk return scenario. But remember, this is rarely a "fair fight." Small business owners only infrequently raise equity capital, while investors do so every day. The latter prefer staging their commitments, thereby managing their risk and preserving their options. Numerous potential conflicts exist between users and suppliers of capital, and these require appreciation and managing. The economic consequences can be worth millions to founders. Successful deals are characterized by careful thought and sensitive balance among a range of important issues.

Deal structure can make or break an otherwise sound venture, and the devil is always in the details. The entrepreneur encounters numerous strategic, legal, and other "sand traps" during the fund-raising cycle and needs awareness and skill in coping with them.

While deal making is ultimately a combination of art and science, it is possible to describe some of the characteristics of deals that have proven successful over time:

- They are simple.
- They are robust (they do not fall apart when there are minor deviations from projections).
- They are organic (they are not immutable).
- They take into account the incentives of each party to the deal under a variety of circumstances.
- They provide mechanisms for communications and interpretation.
- They are based primarily on trust rather than on legalese.
- They are not patently unfair.
- They do not make it too difficult to raise additional capital.
- They match the needs of the user of capital with the needs of the supplier.
- They reveal information about each party (e.g., their faith in their abilities to deliver on the promises).
- They allow for the arrival of new information before financing is required.

- They do not preserve discontinuities (e.g., boundary conditions that will evoke dysfunctional behavior on the part of the agents of principals).
- They take into account the fact that it takes time to raise money.

Notes

1. William A. Sahlman's "Note on Financial Contracting: Deals," HBS Note 9-288-014, Harvard Business School, 1987, p. 1, and "A Method for Valuing High-Risk, Long-Term Investment: The Venture Capital Method," Note 9-288-006, Harvard Business School, 1987, have significantly influenced educators, entrepreneurs, and equity investors thinking about deal making.

2. HBS Note 9-288-014, pp. 35–36.

3. HBS Note 9-288-006, p. 56.

4. Ibid., pp. 58–59.

5. Ibid., p. 24.

6. ventureone.com/ii/2Q03FinancingRelease.xls.

7. Jeffry A. Timmons, "Deals and Deal Structuring" lecture, Babson College, Oct. 2002.

8. Bob Thomas, *Walt Disney: An American Original* (New York: Simon and Schuster, 1976), p. 276.

9. Herb Cohen, *You Can Negotiate Anything* (New York: Bantam Books, 1982), p. 15.

10. Ibid., p. 16.

11. Roger Fisher and William Ury, *Getting to Yes* (New York: Penguin Books, 1991), p. xvii.

12. See, for example, H. M. Hoffman and J. Blakey, "You Can Negotiate with Venture Capitalists," *Harvard Business Review*, March–April 1987, pp. 16–24.

13. Fisher and Ury, *Getting to Yes*, p. xviii.

14. Paul B. Brown and Michael S. Hopkins, "How to Negotiate Practically Anything," *Inc.*, Feb. 1989, p. 35.

15. Jeffry A. Timmons, "Deals and Deal Structuring" lecture, Babson College, Oct. 2002.

CHAPTER 7

OBTAINING
DEBT CAPITAL

"Leveraging a company is like driving your car with a sharp stick pointed at your heart through the steering wheel. As long as the road is smooth it works fine. But hit one bump in the road and you may be dead."

— WARREN BUFFET

A Cyclical Pattern: The Good Old Days Returned but Again Faded

For small business owners and their investors, the punishing credit crunch and stagnant equity markets of 1990–1993 gave way to the most robust capital markets in U.S. history into the new millennium. Declining interest rates reached historical lows in 2003 and the credit environment was much friendlier, mimicking the heady days of precrash 1987. Not only did interest rates decline, the availability of bank loans and competition among banks increased dramatically from the dormant days of the early 1990s.

The improved credit environment led to a greater marketing awareness by lenders of the potential represented by the growth companies in the new entrepreneurial economy. Bank presidents and loan officers were aggressively seeking out entrepreneurial companies as prospective clients. They worked with local universities and entrepreneurial associations to sponsor seminars, workshops, and business fairs, all to cultivate entrepreneurial customers. This was a welcome change in the credit climate for entrepreneurs. A smaller and less severe credit crunch (even with extremely low interest rates) began in 2000 and increased into 2002, but it is important to remember that the availability of credit is cyclical and the fundamentals of credit don't change that much. As the economy has emerged from recession in 2003 the credit environment has improved also. Low rates and high availability makes debt financing an attractive capital alternative.

A Word of Caution

Even if a credit environment is favorable, history suggests that this can and will change, sometimes suddenly. Entrepreneurs who are mindful of this can appreciate just how onerous borrowing can become. What can be expected when a credit climate reverses itself? For one thing, personal guarantees* come back. Even the most creditworthy companies with enviable records for timely repayment of interest and principal could be asked to provide personal guarantees by the owners. The following is a phenomenon that can be viewed as a perversion of the debt capital markets. As a credit crunch becomes more severe, banks face their own illiquidity and insolvency problems, which might result in the failure of more banks (as happened in the 1990s). To cope with their own balance-sheet dissipation, banks can call the best loans first. Thousands of high-quality smaller companies would be stunned and debilitated by such actions. It is also true that with less competition among banks, pricing and terms can become more onerous as the economy continues in a period of credit tightening. Debt reduction could then become a dominant financial strategy of small and large companies alike. Robert Frost said, "A bank is a place where they lend you an umbrella in fair weather and ask for it back when it begins to rain."

*The entrepreneur personally guarantees that the loan will be repaid. If the company fails, the entrepreneur is personally liable to repay the loan from her or his personal assets (which can lead to personal bankruptcy on top of entrepreneurial failure).

The Lender's Perspective

Lenders have always been wary capital providers. Understandably, since banks may earn as little as a 1 percent net profit on total assets, they are especially sensitive to the possibility of a loss. Imagine writing off a $1 million loan to a small company. The bank has to turn around and lend and be repaid an incremental $100 million in profitable loans just to recover that loss. Yet lending institutions are businesses and seek to grow and improve profitability as well. They can do this only if they find and bet on successful, young, growing companies. Historically, points and fees charged for making a loan have been a major contributor to bank profitability.

Sources of Debt Capital[1]

The principal sources[2] of borrowed capital for growing businesses are trade credit, commercial banks, finance companies, factors, and leasing companies. The advantages and disadvantages[3] of these sources, summarized in Exhibit 7.1, are basically determined by such obvious dimensions as the interest rate or cost of capital, the key terms, conditions and covenants, and the fit with the owner's situation and the company's needs at the time. How good a deal you can strike is a function of your relative bargaining position and the competitiveness among the alternatives. What is ultimately most important, given a deal at or above an acceptable threshold, is the person with whom you will be dealing, rather than the amount, terms, or institution. In other words, you will be better off seeking the right banker (or other provider of capital) than just the right bank. Once again, the industry and market characteristics, stage, and health of the firm in terms of cash flow, debt coverage, and collateral are central to the evaluation process. Clearly the profitable small business with a smart growth plan has great advantages in gaining debt capital. And remember, debt capital is almost always cheaper than equity capital. Finally, an enduring question entrepreneurs ask is, What is bankable—how much money can I expect to borrow based on my balance sheet? Exhibit 7.2 summarizes some general guidelines in answer to this question. Since most loans and lines of credit are asset-based loans, knowing the guidelines employed by lenders to determine how much to lend the company is very important. When you observe the percentages of key balance-sheet assets that are often allowable as collateral, note that these are only ranges and will vary from region to region, for different types of businesses, and for stages in the business cycle. For instance, nonperishable consumer goods versus technical products that may have considerable risk of obsolescence would be treated very differently in making a loan collateral computation. If the company already has significant debt and has pledged all of its assets, there may not be a lot of room for negotiations. A bank with full collateral in hand for a company having cash-flow problems is unlikely to give up such a position in order to enable the company to attract another lender, even though the collateral is more than enough to meet these guidelines.

Trade Credit[4]

Trade credit is a major source of short-term funds for small businesses. In fact, trade credit represents 30–40 percent of the current liabilities of nonfinancial companies, with generally higher percentages in smaller companies. Trade credit is reflected on the balance sheets as accounts payable, or sales payable—trade. If a small business is able to buy goods and services and be given, or take, thirty, sixty, or ninety days to pay

Exhibit 7.1 Debt Financing Sources for Types of Business

Source	Available to Small Business?
Trade credit	Yes, with a history of sound relationships
Finance companies	Yes, with strong equity
Commercial banks	Yes (if assets are available)
Factors	Depends on nature of the customers
Leasing companies	Yes, depending on machinery and equipment mix
Mutual savings banks	Depends on strength of personal guarantee
Insurance companies	Rare, except alongside venture capital

for them, that business has essentially obtained a loan of 30 to 90 days. Many small and new businesses are able to obtain such trade credit when no other form of debt financing is available to them. Suppliers offer trade credit as a way of enticing new customers, and often build the bad-debt risk into their prices. Additionally, channel partners who supply trade credit often do so with more industry-specific knowledge than can be obtained by commercial banks.[5] The ability of a small business to obtain trade credit depends on the quality and reputation of its management and the relationships it establishes with its suppliers. A word of warning: continued late payment or nonpayment may cause suppliers to cut off shipments or ship only on a COD basis—and you develop a reputation, both formally through credit reports and informally through word of mouth, very quickly. A key to keeping trade credit open is to pay continually, even if not the full amount. Also, the real cost of using trade credit can be very high—for example, the loss of discounts for prompt payment. Because the cost of trade credit is seldom expressed as an annual amount, it should be analyzed carefully, and you should shop for the best terms. Trade credit may take some of the following forms: extended credit terms; special or seasonal datings, where a supplier ships goods in advance of the purchaser's peak selling season and accepts payment 90–120 days later during the season; inventory on consignment, not requiring payment until sold; and loan or lease of equipment.

Exhibit 7.2 What Is Bankable? Specific Lending Criteria

Security	Credit Capacity
Accounts receivable	70–85% of those less than 90 days of acceptable receivables
Inventory	20–70% depending on obsolescence risk and salability
Equipment	70–80% of market value (less if specialized)
Chattel mortgage	80% or more of auction appraisal value
Conditional sales contract	60–70% or more of purchase price
Plant improvement loan	60–80% of appraised value or cost

Source: Updated from Jeffry A. Timmons, *Financing and Planning the New Venture* (Acton, MA: Brick House Publishing, 1990), Table 1, p. 33.

Commercial Bank Financing

Commercial banks prefer to lend to existing businesses that have a track record of sales, profits, satisfied customers, and a current backlog. Their concern about the high failure rates in new businesses can make them less than enthusiastic about making loans to such firms. They like to be lower-risk lenders, which is consistent with their profit margins. For their protection, they look first to positive cash flow and then to collateral, and in new and young businesses (depending on the credit environment) they are likely to require personal guarantees of the owners. Like equity investors, they place great weight on the quality of the management team. Notwithstanding these factors, certain banks do, rarely, make loans to small businesses that have strong equity financings. This has been especially true in such centers of entrepreneurial and venture capital activity as Silicon Valley, Boston, and Los Angeles.

Commercial banks are the primary source of debt capital for existing (not new) businesses. Small business loans may be handled by a bank's small business loan department or through credit scoring (where credit approval is done "by the numbers"). It is worth noting that your personal credit history will also impact the credit scoring matrix. Larger loans may require the approval of a loan committee. If a loan exceeds the limits of a local bank, part of (or the entire) loan amount will be offered to "correspondent" banks in neighboring communities and nearby financial centers. This correspondent network enables the smaller banks in rural areas to handle loans that otherwise could not be made.

Most of the loans made by commercial banks are for one year or less. Some of these loans are unsecured, while receivables, inventories, or other assets secure others. Commercial banks also make a large number of intermediate-term loans (or term loans) with a maturity of one to five years. On about 90 percent of these term loans, the banks require collateral, generally consisting of stocks, machinery, equipment, and real estate. Most term loans are retired by systematic, but not necessarily equal, payments over the life of the loan. Apart from real estate mortgages and loans guaranteed by the SBA or a similar organization, commercial banks make few loans with maturities greater than five years.

Banks also offer a number of services to the small business, such as computerized payroll preparation, letters of credit, international services, lease financing, and money market accounts.

There are now approximately 6,500 commercial banks in the United States. A complete listing of banks can be found, arranged by states, in the *American Bank Directory* (McFadden Business Publications), published semiannually.

Line of Credit Loans

A line of credit is a formal or informal agreement between a bank and a borrower concerning the maximum loan a bank will allow the borrower for a one-year period. Often the bank will charge a fee (usually a percentage of the line of credit) for a definite commitment to make the loan when requested. Line of credit funds are used for such seasonal financings as inventory buildup and receivable financing. These two items are often the largest and most financeable items on a venture's balance sheet. It is general practice to repay these loans from the sales and reduction of short-term assets that they financed. Lines of credit could be unsecured, or the bank may require a pledge of inventory, receivables, equipment, or other acceptable assets. Unsecured lines of credit have no lien on any asset of the borrower and no priority over any trade creditor, but the banks may require that all debt to the principals and stockholders of the company be subordinated to the line of credit debt. The line of credit is executed through a series of renewable ninety-day notes. The renewable ninety-day note is the more common practice, and the bank will expect the borrower to pay off his or her open loan within a year and to hold a zero loan balance for one to two months. This is known as "resting the line" or "cleaning up." Commercial banks may also generally require that a borrower maintain a checking account at the bank with a minimum ("compensating") balance of 5–10 percent of the outstanding loan.

For a large, financially sound company, the interest rates for a "prime risk" line of credit will be quoted at the prime rate or at a premium over LIBOR (London Interbank Offered Rate). Eurodollars (American dollars held outside of the United States) are most actively traded here, and banks use Eurodollars as the "last" dollars to balance the funding of its loan portfolio. Thus, LIBOR represents the marginal cost of funds for a bank. A small firm may be required to pay a higher rate. It should be noted that the true interest calculations need to take into consideration the multiple fees that may be added to the loan. Any compensating-balance or resting-the-line requirements or other fees will also increase effective interest rates.

Time-Sales Finance

Many dealers or manufacturers who offer installment payment terms to purchasers of their equipment cannot themselves finance installment or conditional sales contracts. In such situations, they sell and assign the installment contract to a bank or sales finance company. (Some very large manufacturers do their own financing through captive finance companies. Most very small retailers merely refer their customer install-ment contracts to sales finance companies, which provide much of this financing, and on more flexible terms.)

From the manufacturer's or dealer's point of view, time-sales finance is, in effect, a way of obtaining short-term financing from long-term installment accounts receivable. From the purchaser's point of view, it is a way of financing the purchase of new equipment.

Under time-sales financing, the bank purchases installment contracts at a discount from their full value and takes as security an assignment of the manufacturer/dealer's interest in the conditional sales contract. In addition, the bank's financing of installment note receivables includes recourse to the seller in the event of loan default by the purchaser. Thus, the bank has the payment obligation of the equipment purchaser, the manufacturer/dealer's security interest in the equipment purchased, and recourse to the manufacturer/dealer in the event of default. The bank also withholds a portion of the payment (5 percent or more) as a dealer reserve until the note is paid. Since the reserve becomes an increasing percentage of the note as the contract is paid off, an arrange-ment is often made when multiple contracts are financed to ensure that the reserve against all contracts will not exceed 20 percent or so.

The purchase price of equipment under a sales financing arrangement includes a "time-sales price differential" (e.g., an increase to cover the discount, typically 6–10 percent) taken by the bank that does the financing. Collection of the installments may be made directly by the bank or indirectly through the manufacturer/dealer.

Term Loans

Bank term loans are generally made for periods of one to five years, and may be unsecured or secured. Most of the basic features of bank term loans are the same for secured and unsecured loans.

Term loans provide needed growth capital to companies. They are also a substitute for a series of short-term loans made with the hope of renewal by both the borrower and bank. Banks make these generally on the basis of predictability of positive cash flow.

Term loans have three distinguishing features: (1) banks make them for periods of up to five years (and occasionally more); (2) periodic repayment is required; and (3) term loan agreements are designed to fit the special needs and requirements of the borrower (e.g., payments can be smaller at the beginning of a loan term and larger at the end).

Because term loans do not mature for a number of years, during which time there could be a significant change in the situation and fortunes of the borrower, the bank must carefully evaluate the prospects and management of the borrowing company. Even the protection afforded by initially strong assets can be wiped out by several years of heavy losses. Term lenders place particular stress on the entrepreneurial and managerial abilities of the borrowing company. The bank will also carefully consider such things as the long-range prospects of the company and its industry, its present and projected profitability, and its ability to generate the cash required to meet the loan payments, as shown by past performance. Pricing for a term loan may be higher, reflecting a perceived higher risk from the longer term.

To lessen the risks involved in term loans, a bank will require some restrictive covenants in the loan agreement. These covenants might prohibit additional borrowing, merger of the company, payment of dividends, sales of assets, increased salaries to the owners, and the like. Also, the bank will probably require financial covenants to provide early warning of deterioration of the business, like debt to equity and cash flow to interest coverage.

Chattel Mortgages and Equipment Loans

Assigning an appropriate possession (chattel) as security is a common way of making secured term loans. The chattel is any machinery, equipment, or business property that is made the collateral of a loan in the same way as a mortgage on real estate. The chattel remains with the borrower unless there is default, in which case the chattel goes to the bank. Generally, credit against machinery and equipment is restricted primarily to new or highly serviceable and resalable used items.

It should be noted that in many states, loans that used to be chattel mortgages are now executed through the security agreement forms of the Uniform Commercial Code (UCC). However, chattel mortgages are still used in many places (for, example, moving vehicles like tractors or cranes), and, from custom, many lenders continue to use that term even though the loans are executed through the UCC's security agreements. The term of a *chattel mortgage* is typically from one to five years; some have longer terms.

Conditional Sales Contracts

Conditional sales contracts are used to finance a substantial portion of the new equipment purchased by businesses. Under a sales contract, the buyer agrees to purchase a piece of equipment, makes a nominal down payment, and pays the balance in installments over a period of from one to five years. Until the payment is complete, the seller holds title to the equipment. Hence, the sale is conditional upon the buyer's completing the payments.

A sales contract is financed by a bank that has recourse to the seller should the purchaser default on the loan. This makes it more difficult to finance a purchase of a good piece of used equipment at an auction. No recourse to the seller is available if the equipment is purchased at an auction; the bank would have to sell the equipment if the loan goes bad. Occasionally, a firm seeking financing on existing and new equipment will sell some of its equipment to a dealer and repurchase it, together with new equipment, in order to get a conditional sales contract financed by a bank.

The effective rate of interest on a conditional sales contract is high, as much as 15–18 percent if the effect of installment features is considered. The purchaser/borrower should thus make sure that the interest payment is covered by increased productivity and profitability resulting from the new equipment.

Plant Improvement Loans

Loans made to finance improvements to business properties and plants are called plant improvement loans. These intermediate- and long-term loans are generally secured by a mortgage (or a second mortgage) on that part of the property or plant that is being improved.

Commercial Finance Companies

The commercial bank is generally the lender of choice for a business. From whom does a business seek loans when the bank says no? Commercial finance companies, which aggressively seek borrowers, are a good option. They frequently loan money to companies that do not have positive cash flow, although they will not make loans to companies unless they consider them viable risks. In tighter credit economies, finance companies are generally more accepting of risk than banks.

The primary factors in a bank's loan decision are the continuing successful operation of a business and its generation of more than enough cash to repay a loan. By contrast, commercial finance companies lend against the liquidation value of assets (receivables, inventory, equipment) that it understands, knows how and where to sell, and whose liquidation value is sufficient to repay the loan. It should be noted that banks today own many of the leading finance companies. The good news here is that, as a borrower gains financial strength and a track record, transfer to more attractive bank financing can be easier. For the small business owner, this transition can be initiated by a growth plan that engages the lending capabilities of these institutions. You would be wise to study the lending habits of your current relationships to assess their appetite.

In the case of inventories or equipment, liquidation value is the amount that could be realized from an auction or quick sale. Finance companies will generally not lend against receivables more than 90 days old, federal or state government agency receivables (against which it is very difficult to perfect a lien—and they are slow payers), or any receivables whose collection is contingent on the performance of a delivered product. Because of the liquidation criteria, finance companies prefer readily resalable inventory items such as electronic components, or metal in such commodity forms as billets or standard shapes. Generally, a finance company will not accept inventory as collateral unless it also has receivables. As for equipment loans, these are made only by certain finance companies and against such standard equipment as lathes, milling machines, and the like. Finance companies, like people, have items in which they are more comfortable and therefore would extend more credit against certain kinds of collateral. How much of the value of collateral will a finance company lend? Generally, 70–90 percent of acceptable receivables under 90 days old, 20–65 percent or even 70 percent of the liquidation value of raw materials and/or finished goods inventory that are not obsolete or damaged, and 60–80 percent of the liquidation value of equipment, as determined by an appraiser. Receivables and inventory loans are for one year, while equipment loans are for three to seven years.

All of these loans have tough prepayment penalties: finance companies do not want to be immediately replaced by banks when a borrower has improved its credit image. Generally, finance companies require a three-year commitment to do business with them, with prepayment fees if this provision is not complied with.

The data required for a loan from a finance company includes all that would be provided to a bank, plus additional details for the assets being used as collateral. For receivables financing, this includes detailed aging of receivables (and payables) and historical data on sales, returns, or deductions (all known as dilution), and collections.

For inventory financing, it includes details on the items in inventory, how long they have been there, and their rate of turnover. Requests for equipment loans should be accompanied by details on the date of purchase, cost of each equipment item, and appraisals, which are generally always required. These appraisals must be made by acceptable (to the lender) outside appraisers.

The advantage of dealing with a commercial finance company is that it will make loans that banks will not, and it can be flexible in lending arrangements. The price a finance company exacts for this is an interest rate anywhere from 0 to 6 percent over that charged by a bank, prepayment penalties, and, in the case of receivables loans, recourse to the borrower for unpaid collateralized receivables. Because of their greater risk taking and asset-based lending, finance companies usually place a larger reporting and monitoring burden on the borrowing firm in order to stay on top of the receivables and inventory serving as loan collateral. Personal guarantees will generally be required from the principals of the business (sometimes defined as more than 5 percent ownership, but this is negotiable). A finance company or bank will generally reserve the right to reduce the percentage of the value lent against receivables or inventory if it gets nervous about the borrower's survivability.

Factoring

Factoring is a form of accounts receivable financing. However, instead of borrowing and using receivables as collateral, the receivables are sold, at a discounted value, to a person or firm called a factor. Factoring is accomplished on a discounted value of the receivables pledged. Invoices that do not meet the factor's credit standard will not be accepted as collateral. (Receivables more than 90 days old are not normally accepted.) A bank may inform the purchaser of goods that the account has been assigned to the bank, and payments are made directly to the bank, which credits them to the borrower's account. This is called a notification plan. Alternatively, the borrower may collect the accounts as usual and pay off the bank loan; this is a nonnotification plan.

Factoring can make it possible for a company to secure a loan that it might not otherwise get. The loan can be increased as sales and receivables grow. However, factoring can be expensive, and trade creditors sometimes regard factoring as evidence of a company in financial difficulty, except in certain industries.

In a standard factoring arrangement, the factor buys the client's receivables outright, without recourse, as soon as the client creates them by shipment of goods to customers. Although the factor has recourse to the borrowers for returns, errors in pricing, and so on, the factor assumes the risk of bad debt losses that develop from receivables it approves and purchases. Many factors, however, provide factoring only on a recourse basis.

Cash is made available to the client as soon as proof is provided (old-line factoring) or on the average due date of the invoices (maturity factoring). With maturity factoring, the company can often obtain a loan of about 90 percent of the money a factor has agreed to pay on a maturity date. Most factoring arrangements are for one year.

Factoring can also be on a recourse basis. In this circumstance, the borrower must replace unpaid receivables after 90 days with new current receivables to allow the borrowings to remain at the same level. If you are growing, replacing receivables is usually not a problem.

Factoring fits some businesses better than others. For a business that has annual sales volume in excess of $300,000 and a net worth over $50,000 that sells on normal credit terms to a customer base that is 75 percent credit rated, factoring is a real option. Factoring has become almost traditional in such industries as textiles, furniture manufacturing, clothing manufacturing, toys, shoes, and plastics.

The same data required from a business for a receivable loan from a bank is required by a factor. Because a factor is buying receivables with no recourse, it will carefully analyze the quality and value of a prospective client's receivables. It will want a detailed aging of receivables plus historical data on bad debts, returns, and allowances. It will also investigate the credit history of customers to whom its client sells and establish credit limits for each customer. The business client can receive factoring of customer receivables only up to the limits so set.

The cost of financing receivables through factoring is higher than that of borrowing from a bank or a finance company. The factor is assuming the credit risk, doing credit investigations and collections, and advancing funds. A factor generally charges up to 2 percent of the total sales factored as a service charge. There is also an interest charge for money advanced to a business, usually 2–6 percent above prime. A larger, established business borrowing great sums would command a better interest rate than the small borrower with a one-time, short-term need. Finally, factors withhold a reserve of 5–10 percent of the receivables purchased.

Factoring is not the cheapest way to obtain capital, but it does quickly turn receivables into cash. For a growth-oriented company, factors can provide valuable fuel. Moreover, although more expensive than accounts receivable financing, factoring saves its users credit agency fees, salaries of credit and collection personnel, and maybe bad debt write-offs. Factoring also provides credit information on collection services that may be better than the borrower's as they approve credit from many suppliers.

Leasing Companies

The leasing industry has grown substantially in recent years, and lease financing has become an important source of medium-term financing for businesses. There are about 700 to 800 leasing companies in the United States. In addition, many commercial banks and finance companies have leasing departments. Some leasing companies handle a wide variety of equipment, while others specialize in certain types of equipment—machine tools, electronic test equipment, and the like.

Common and readily resalable items such as automobiles and trucks and office furniture can be leased by both new and existing businesses. Generally, industrial equipment leases have a term of three to five years, but in some cases may run longer. There can also be lease renewal options for 3–5 percent per year of the original equipment value. Leases are usually structured to return the entire cost of the leased equipment plus finance charges to the lessor, although some so-called operating leases do not, over their term, produce revenues equal to or greater than the price of the leased equipment. Typically, an up-front payment is required of about 10 percent of the value of the item being leased. The interest rate on equipment leasing may be more or less than other forms of financing, depending on the equipment leased, the credit of the lessee, and the time of year.

Leasing credit criteria are very similar to those used by commercial banks for equipment loans. Primary considerations are the value of the equipment leased, the justification of the lease, and the lessee's projected cash flow over the lease term.

Should a business lease equipment? Leasing has certain advantages. It enables a young or growing company to conserve cash, and can reduce its requirements for equity capital. Leasing can also be a tax advantage, because payments can be deducted over a shorter period than depreciation.

Finally, leasing provides the flexibility of returning equipment after the lease period if it is no longer needed or if it has become technologically obsolete. This can be a particular advantage to companies in high-technology industries.

Leasing may or may not improve a company's balance sheet, because accounting practice currently requires that the value of the equipment acquired in a capital lease be reflected there. Operating leases, however, do not appear on the balance sheet. Generally speaking, this is an issue of economic rather than legal ownership. If the economic risk is primarily with the lessee, it must be capitalized and therefore goes on the balance sheet along with the corresponding debt. Depreciation also follows the risk, along with the corresponding tax benefits. It should be noted that start-ups that don't need such tax relief should be able to acquire more favorable terms with an operating lease.

Before the Loan Decision[6]

Choosing a bank and, more specifically, a banker is one of the more important decisions a new or young business will make. (See Exhibit 7.3.) A good lender relationship can sometimes mean the difference between the life and death of a business during difficult times. There have been cases where, other things being equal, one bank has called its

Exhibit 7.3 What to Look for in a Bank

- **Banking knowledge:** Few bankers will intentionally lead you astray. But Dan Lang, co-owner of Nature's Warehouse, a $6 million baked-goods business in Sacramento, discovered that some bankers have a tighter grip than others on what's possible in a given situation. Lang and his partner met with lending officers at several banks to try to get $1 million in financing to help buy Nature's Warehouse. But only one, the lending officer at Sacramento Commercial Bank, "said right away he could do it as a ten-year SBA loan. Without hesitating, he knew what he could and couldn't do."
- **Sense of urgency:** "Banker's hours" may be a fading notion, but a CEO's and a banker's ideas of a "quick turnaround" are often days, even weeks, apart. Tom Kinder, co-owner of Pure Patience, a bedding-products mail-order business in Sharon, Vermont, found that his bankers at Vermont National Bank were able—and extremely willing—to meet his compressed timetable for a $100,000 loan. Kinder says he even got evening calls at home, updating him on the progress. One of the reasons for the time-perception difference is that the bank starts timing when all the data they need is in their hands, while the entrepreneur starts counting as soon as the first call is made!
- **Teaching talent:** Many bankers can't—or don't want to—articulate what they expect from customers and how the bank makes its decisions. But Dwight Mulch, president of Preferred Products Corp., a building-materials distributor in Burlington, Iowa, says he gets both types of information from his lending officer at First Star Bank and has benefited greatly. "He practically led me around by the nose. He showed me what to put in the plan, and he still tells me how the system works," says Mulch.
- **Industry knowledge:** Whatever industry you're in, it helps to have a banker who has had some exposure to your type of business, says Dave Sanger, president of Resource Solution Group, a computer-consulting business in Southfield, Michigan. Sanger's lending officer at Manufacturer's Bank in Detroit "knows we don't have the same kind of assets as a retailer or a manufacturer," Sanger says, "and she knows the terminology."
- **Financial stability:** Given a choice, Kevin Whalen, chief financial advisor of Twin Modal, Inc., a Minneapolis transportation-brokerage firm, didn't pick the bank that was offering the most aggressive deal. And it's a good thing too, he says: "that bank has had real problems with regulators and has pulled way back." Before selecting Marquette Bank, Whalen, a former banker himself, did spreadsheet comparisons of several banks, comparing returns on assets, capital-to-asset ratios, and so on. "I felt that in the long run, we'd be better off with the most conservative bank around."
- **Manager with backbone:** Banks have policies, notes Mike Walker, president of Walker Communications Inc., a public relations firm in Scottsdale, Arizona, "but you want to have a manager with the courage to override them if it makes sense to do so." Walker's branch manager at First Interstate Bank of Arizona, for instance, allows him to draw on checks immediately after they're deposited and often acts as a troubleshooter for him within the bank. "I don't know what the manual says," offers Walker, "but I think you need somebody who can take a stand." (This is true when the request is reasonable.)

Source: Used with permission from "What to Look for in a Bank." As seen in the July 1992 issue of *Inc.* magazine. Copyright © 1992 by Gruner & Jahr USA Publishing. All rights reserved.

loans to a struggling business, causing it to go under, and another bank has stayed with its loans and helped a business to survive and prosper. (Although we refer specifically to banks and banking relationships, much of the following discussion of lending practices and decisions applies as well to commercial finance company lenders.) However, it should be recognized that many large banks, when considering relatively small loans (under $2 million), rely mostly on credit scoring to decide whether credit can be granted.

Those banks that will not make such loans generally cite the lack of operating track record as the primary reason for their refusal. Growth, based on a history of operating success, is one of the favored reasons for lending. Lenders pay particular attention to firms with seasoned management teams who are backed by investors with whom they have had prior relationships and whose judgment they trust.

Exhibit 7.4 offers guidelines for the entrepreneur and his or her management team as to the preliminary steps they should take in asking for a loan. Because of the importance of a banking relationship, an entrepreneur should shop around before choosing a banker or other lender. The criteria for selecting a bank should be based on more than just loan interest rates. Equally important, entrepreneurs should not wait until they have a dire need for funds to try to establish a banking relationship. The choice of a bank and the development of a banking relationship should begin when you do not urgently need the money. When an entrepreneur faces a near-term financial crisis, the venture's financial statements are at their worst and the banker has good cause to wonder about management's financial and planning skills—all to the detriment of the entrepreneur's chance of getting a loan.

G. B. Baty and J. M. Stancill describe some of the factors that are especially important to an entrepreneur in selecting a bank.[7] The bank selected should be big enough to service a venture's foreseeable loans but not so large as to be relatively indifferent to your business. Banks vary greatly in their desire and capacity to work with small firms. Some banks have special small business loan officers. Other banks see such new venture loans as merely bad risks. Does the bank tend to call or reduce its loans to small businesses that have problems? When they have less capital to lend, will they cut back on small business loans and favor their older, more solid customers? Are they imaginative, creative, and

Exhibit 7.4 Key Steps in Obtaining a Loan

Before choosing and approaching a banker or other lender, the entrepreneur and his/her management team should go through the following steps in preparing to ask for a loan.

- Decide how much growth they want, and how fast they want to grow, observing the dictum that financing follows strategy.
- Determine how much money they require, when they need to have it, and when they can pay it back. To this end, they must:
  —develop a schedule of operating and asset needs
  —prepare a real-time cash-flow projection
  —decide how much capital they need
  —specify how they will use the funds they borrow
- Revise and update the "corporate profile" in their business plan. This should consist of:
  —the core ingredients of the plan in the form of an executive summary
  —a history of the firm
  —summaries of the financial results of the past three years
  —succinct descriptions of their markets and products
  —a description of their operations
  —statements of cash flow and financial requirements
  —descriptions of the key managers, owners, and directors
  —a rundown of the key strategies, facts, and logic that guide them in growing the corporation
- Identify potential sources for the type of debt they seek, and the amount, rate, terms, *and conditions* they seek.
- Select a bank or other lending institution, solicit interest, and prepare a presentation.
- Prepare a written loan request.
- Present their case, negotiate, and then close the deal.
- After the loan is granted, it is important that the borrowers maintain an effective relationship with the lending officer.

Source: Jeffry A. Timmons, *Financing and Planning the New Venture* (Acton, MA: Brick House Publishing, 1990), pp. 82–83.

helpful when a venture has a problem? To quote Baty, "Do they just look at your balance sheet and faint or do they try to suggest constructive financial alternatives?"

Finally, ask for small business references from their list of borrowers and talk to the entrepreneurs of those firms. Throughout all of these contacts and discussions, check out particular loan officers as well as the viability of the bank itself—after all, the officers are a major determinant of how the bank will deal with you and your venture.

What the Banker Wants to Know[8]

You first need to describe the business and its industry. Exhibit 7.5 suggests how a banker "sees a company" from what the entrepreneur might say. What are you going to do with the money? Does the use of the loan make business sense? Should some or all of the money required be equity capital rather than debt? For most businesses, lenders do not like to see total debt-to-equity ratios greater than one. The answers to these questions will also determine the type of loan (e.g., line of credit or term).

1. How much do you need? You must be prepared to justify the amount requested and describe how the debt fits into an overall plan for financing and developing the business. Further, the amount of the loan should have enough of a cushion to allow for unexpected developments.

2. When and how will you pay it back? This is an important question. Short-term loans for seasonal inventory buildups or for financing receivables are easier to obtain than long-term loans, especially for early-stage businesses. How the loan will be repaid is the bottom-line question. Presumably you are borrowing money to finance activity that will throw off enough cash to repay the loan. What is your contingency plan if things go wrong? Can you describe such risks and indicate how you will deal with them?

3. What is the secondary source of repayment? Are there assets or a guarantor of means?

4. When do you need the money? If you need the money tomorrow, forget it. You are a poor planner and manager. On the other hand, if you need the money next month or the month after, you have demonstrated an ability to plan ahead, and you have given the banker time to investigate and process a loan application. Typically, it is difficult to get a lending decision in less than three weeks (some smaller banks still have once-a-month credit meetings).

One of the best ways for all entrepreneurs to answer these questions is from a well-prepared business plan. This plan should contain projections of cash flow, profit and loss, and balance sheets that will demonstrate the need for a loan and how it can be repaid. Particular attention will be given by the lender to the value of the assets and the cash flow of the business, and to such financial ratios as current assets to current

Exhibit 7.5 Bankerese: How Your Banker Interprets the Income Statement

Sales	What do you sell?
	Whom do you sell to?
• Cost of Goods	How do you buy?
	What do you buy?
	Whom do you buy from?
Gross Margin	Are you a supermarket or a boutique?
• Selling	How do you sell and distribute the product?
• G & A	How much overhead and support is needed to operate?
• R & D	How much is reinvested in the product?
Operating Margins	How many dollars are available before financing costs?
• Interest Expense	How big is this fixed nut?
• Profit Before Taxes	Do you make money?
• Taxes	Corporation, Sub S, LLC, or LLP?
• Profit After Taxes	
• Dividends/Withdrawals	How much and to whom?
	How much money is left in the company?

Source: This exhibit was created by Kathie S. Stevens and Leslie Charm as part of a class discussion in the Entrepreneurial Finance course at Babson College, and is part of a presentation titled "Cash Is King, Assets Are Queen, and Everybody Is Looking for an Ace in the Hole." Ms. Stevens is a former chief lending officer and credit committee member for a Boston bank.

liabilities, gross margins, net worth to debt, accounts receivable and payable periods, inventory turns, and net profit to sales. The ratios for the borrower's venture will be compared to averages for competing firms to see how the potential borrower measures up to them.

For an existing business, the lender will want to review prior years' financial statements prepared or audited by a CPA, a list of aged receivables and payables, the turnover of inventory, and lists of key customers and creditors. The lender will also want to know that all tax payments are current. Finally, he or she will need to know details of fixed assets and any liens on receivables, inventory, or fixed assets.

You should regard your contacts with the bank as a sales mission and provide required data promptly and in a form that can be readily understood. The better the material you can supply to demonstrate your business credibility, the easier and faster it will be to obtain a positive lending decision. You should also ask, early on, to meet with the banker's boss. This can go a long way to help obtain financing. Remember you need to build a relationship with a bank, not just a banker.

The Lending Decision

One of the significant changes in today's lending environment is the centralized lending decision. Traditionally, loan officers have had as much as several million dollars of lending authority and could make loans to small companies. Besides the company's creditworthiness as determined by analysis of its past results via the balance sheet, income statement, cash flow, and collateral, the lender's assessment of the character and reputation of the entrepreneur was central to the decision. As loan decisions are made increasingly by loan committees or credit scoring, this face-to-face part of the decision process has given way to deeper analysis of the company's business plan, cash-flow drivers and dissipaters, competitive environment, and cushion for loan recovery given the firm's game plan and financial structure.

The implication for entrepreneurs is a demanding one: you can no longer rely solely on your salesmanship and a good relationship with your loan officer for favorable lending decisions. You, or the key team member, must prepare the necessary analysis and documentation to convince people (whom you may never meet) that the loan will be repaid. You also need to know the financial ratios and criteria used to compare your loan request with industry norms and to defend the analysis. Such a presentation can facilitate and quicken approval of a loan, because it gives your relationship manager the ammunition to defend your loan request.

After the Loan Decision[9]

Loan Restrictions

A loan agreement defines the terms and conditions under which a lender provides capital. With it, lenders do two things: try to assure repayment of the loan as agreed, and try to protect their position as creditor. Within the loan agreement (as in investment agreements) there are negative and positive covenants. Negative covenants are restrictions on the borrower—for example, no further additions to the borrower's total debt, no pledge to others of assets of the borrower, and no payment of dividends or limitation on owners' salaries.

Positive covenants define what the borrower must do. Some examples are maintenance of some minimum net worth or working capital, prompt payment of all federal and state taxes, adequate insurance on key people and property, repayment of the loan and interest according to the terms of the agreement, and provision to the lender of periodic financial statements and reports.

Some of these restrictions can hinder a company's growth—for example, a flat restriction on further borrowing. Such a borrowing limit is often based on the borrower's assets at the time of the loan. However, rather than stipulating an initially fixed limit, the loan agreement should recognize that as a business grows and increases its total assets and net worth, it will need and be able to carry the additional debt required to sustain its growth; however, banks (especially in tighter credit periods) will still put maximums after allowed credit, as this gives themselves another opportunity to recheck the loan. Similarly, covenants that require certain minimums on working capital or current ratios may be very difficult, for example, for a highly seasonal business to maintain at all times of the year. Careful analysis of past monthly financial statements and your growth pro forma statements can indicate whether such a covenant can be met.

Covenants to Look For

Before borrowing money, an entrepreneur should decide what sorts of restrictions or covenants are acceptable. Attorneys and accountants of the company should be consulted before any loan papers are signed. Some covenants are negotiable (however, like many elements, this changes with the overall credit economy), and an entrepreneur should negotiate to get terms that the venture can live with next year as well as today. Once loan terms are agreed upon and the loan is made, the entrepreneur and the venture will be bound by them. You probably shouldn't accept the loan if the bank:

- Wants to put constraints on your permissible financial ratios
- Would not allow any new borrowing
- Wants a veto on any new management
- Would not allow new products or new directions
- Bars you from acquiring or selling any assets
- Would not allow any new investment or new equipment

Personal Guarantees and the Loan

You can expect to have to personally guarantee a loan:

- If you are undercollateralized
- If there are shareholder loans or lots of "due to" and "due from" officer accounts
- If you have had a poor or erratic performance
- If you have management problems
- If your relationship with your banker is strained
- If you have a new loan officer
- If there is turbulence in the credit markets
- If there has been a wave of bad loans made by the lending institution, and a crackdown is in force
- If there is less understanding of your market

The best ways to avoid personal guarantees are as follows:

- Good to spectacular performance
- Conservative financial management
- Positive cash flow over a sustained period
- Adequate collateral
- Careful management of the balance sheet

Finally, if you already have personally guaranteed loans, here is how to eliminate them:

- Develop a financial plan with performance targets and a timetable.
- Negotiate elimination *up front* when you have some *bargaining* chips, based on certain performance criteria.
- Stay active in the search for backup sources of funds.

Building a Relationship

After obtaining a loan, entrepreneurs should cultivate a close working relationship with their bankers. Too many businesspeople do not see their lending officers until they need a loan. The astute entrepreneur will take a much more active role in keeping a banker informed about the business, thereby improving the chances of obtaining larger loans for expansion, and cooperation from the bank in troubled times.

Some of the things that should be done to build such a relationship are fairly simple.[10] In addition to monthly and annual financial statements, bankers should be sent product news releases and any trade articles about the business or its products. The entrepreneur should invite the banker to the venture's facility, review product development plans and the prospects for the business, and establish a personal relationship with him or her. If this is done, when a new loan is requested, the lending officer will feel better about recommending its approval.

What about bad news? Never surprise a banker with bad news; make sure he or she sees it coming as soon as you do. Unpleasant surprises are a sign that an entrepreneur is not being candid with the banker or that management does not have the business under the proper control. Either conclusion by a banker is damaging to the relationship.

If a future loan payment cannot be met, do not panic and avoid your bankers. On the contrary, visit the bank and explain why the loan payment cannot be made and specify when it will be made. If this is done before the payment due date and if you have a good relationship, the banker may go along. After all, what else can he or she do? If you have convinced a banker of the viability and future growth of a business, the banker really does not want to call a loan and lose a customer to a competitor, or cause bankruptcy. The real key to communicating with a banker is to candidly inform but not to scare. In other words, entrepreneurs must indicate that they are aware of adverse events and have a plan for dealing with them.

To further build credibility with bankers, you should borrow before you need to and then repay the loan. This will establish a track record of reliable repayment. You should also make every effort to meet the financial targets you set for yourself and discussed with your banker. If this cannot be done, there will be an erosion of your credibility, even if the business is growing.

Bankers have a right to expect an entrepreneur to continue to use them as the business grows and prospers, and not to go shopping for a better interest rate. In return, entrepreneurs have the right to expect that their bank will continue to provide them with needed loans, particularly during difficult times when a vacillating loan policy could be dangerous for a business's survival.

What to Do When the Bank Says No

What can you do if the bank turns you down for a loan? Regroup, and review the following questions:

1. Does the company really need to borrow now? Can cash be generated elsewhere? Tighten the belt. Are some expenditures unnecessary? Sharpen the financial pencil: be lean and mean.
2. What does the balance sheet say? Are you growing too fast? Compare yourself to published industry ratios to see if you are on target.
3. Does the bank have a clear and comprehensive understanding of your needs? Did you really get to know your loan officer? Did you do enough homework on the bank's criteria and their likes and dislikes? Was your loan officer too busy to give your borrowing package proper consideration? A loan officer may have 50 to as many as 200 accounts. Is your relationship with the bank on a proper track?
4. Was your written loan proposal realistic? Was it a normal request, or something that differed from the types of proposals the bank usually sees? Did you make a verbal request for a loan, without presenting any written backup?
5. Do you need a new loan officer, or a new bank? If your answers to the above questions put you in the clear, and your written proposal

was realistic, call the head of the commercial loan department and arrange a meeting. Sit down and discuss the history of your loan effort, the facts, and the bank's reasons for turning you down.

6. Who else might provide this financing? (Ask the banker who turned you down.)

In any case, you should be seeing multiple lenders simultaneously to prevent running out of time or money.

Beware of Leverage: The ROE Mirage

According to theory, one can significantly improve return on equity (ROE) by utilizing debt. Thus, the present value of a company would also increase significantly as the company went from a 0 debt-to-equity ratio to 100 percent. On closer examination, however, such an increase in debt only improves the present value (given the 2–8 percent growth rates) shown by 17–26 percent. If the company gets into any trouble at all—and the odds of that happening sooner or later are very high—its options and flexibility become very seriously constrained by the covenants of the senior lenders. Leverage creates an unforgiving capital structure, and the potential additional ROI often is not worth the risk. If the upside is worth risking the loss of the entire company should adversity strike, then go ahead. This is easier said than survived, however.

Ask any entrepreneur who has had to deal with the workout specialists in a bank and you will get a sobering, if not frightening, message: it is hell and you will not want to do it again.

Conclusion

Business cycles impact lending cycles with more or less restrictive behavior. But existing businesses with solid financial performance are better suited for debt capital than start-ups, especially when the economy is emerging from a recession. Managing and orchestrating the banking relationship before and after the loan decision is a key task for entrepreneurs.

Notes

1. This section is drawn from Jeffry A. Timmons, *Financing and Planning the New Venture* (Acton, MA: Brick House Publishing Company, 1990).

2. Ibid., p. 68.

3. Ibid., p. 33.

4. Ibid., pp. 68–80.

5. Neelam Jain, "Monitoring Costs and Trade Credit," *Quarterly Review of Economics and Finance* 41, no. 1 (Spring 2001): pp. 89–111.

6. Ibid., pp. 81–82.

7. G. B. Baty, *Entrepreneurship: Playing to Win* (Reston, VA: Reston Publishing Company, 1974); J. M. Stancill, "Getting the Most from Your Banking Relationship," *Harvard Business Review*, March/April 1980.

8. This section is drawn from Timmons, *Financing and Planning the New Venture*, pp. 85–88.

9. Ibid., pp. 90–94.

10. Baty, *Entrepreneurship: Playing to Win*.

CHAPTER 8

MANAGING RAPID GROWTH*

"Bite off more than you can chew, and then chew it!"
—ROGER BABSON, FOUNDER, BABSON COLLEGE

Inventing New Organizational Paradigms

It is the nimble and fleet-footed entrepreneurial firms that have supplanted the aging giants with new leadership approaches, a passion for value creation, and an obsession with opportunity that has been unbeatable in the marketplace for talent and ideas. These entrepreneurial ventures are the job creators, dinosaur killers, and backbone of the economy.

Because of their innovative nature and competitive breakthroughs, entrepreneurial ventures have demonstrated a remarkable capacity to invent new kinds of organization and management. They have abandoned the organizational practices and structures typical of the industrial giants from the post–World War II era to the 1990s. Larger firms tend to lack creativity and the flexibility to deal with ambiguity and rapid change. Many of them made up for this with rules, structure, hierarchy, and quantitative analysis.

*Special thanks to Ed Marram—entrepreneur, educator, and friend—for his lifelong commitment to studying and leading growing businesses and sharing his knowledge with the authors.

The epitome of this pattern is the Hay System, which by the 1980s became the leading method of defining and grading management jobs in large companies. Scoring high with "Hay points" was the key to more pay, a higher position in the hierarchy, and greater power. The criteria for Hay points include number of people who are direct reports, value of assets under management, sales volume, number of products, square feet of facilities, total size of one's operating and capital budget, and the like. One can easily see how to get ahead in such a system: be bureaucratic, have the most people and the largest budget, increase head count and levels under your control, and think up the largest capital projects. Note that missing in the criteria are all the basic components of entrepreneurship we have seen in this book: value creation, opportunity creation/seeking/seizing, frugality with resources, bootstrapping strategies, staged capital commitments, team building, achieving better fits, and juggling paradoxes.

Contrast the multilayered, hierarchical, military-like levels of control and command that characterize brontosaurus capitalism with the common patterns among entrepreneurial firms: they are flat (often only one or two layers deep), adaptive, and flexible; they look like interlocking circles rather than ladders; they focus on customers and critical missions; they are based on education and influence rather than on rank and power. Entrepreneurs lead more through influence and persuasion, which are derived from knowledge and performance rather than through formal status, position, or seniority. They create a perpetual learning culture. They value people and share the wealth with those who helped create it.

Entrepreneurial Leaders Are Not Administrators or Managers

For the growing business, the general focus is on decisions owner-entrepreneurs make in recognizing and choosing opportunities, allocating resources, motivating employees, and maintaining control—while encouraging the innovative actions that cause a business to grow. The small business owner's challenge is to learn how to dance with elephants without being trampled to death! The ultimate goal of the entrepreneur is to develop the firm to the point where it is able to lead the elephants on the dance floor.

Consider the following quotes from two distinguished business leaders:

> *"MBAs are people in Fortune 500 companies who make careers out of saying no!"*
>
> —Fred Smith, founder, chairman, and CEO of Federal Express

> *"There isn't any business that a Harvard MBA cannot analyze out of existence!"*
>
> —General George Doriot, father of American venture capital and professor at Harvard Business School

Those are profound statements, given the sources. These perceptions also help to explain the stagnancy and eventual demise of brontosaurus capitalism. After all, legions of MBAs in the 1950s, 1960s, 1970s, and early 1980s were taught the brontosaurus model of management. Until the 1980s, virtually all of the cases, problems, and lectures in MBA programs were about large, established companies. That has changed over the last decade as more MBA programs have introduced and expanded entrepreneurial offerings. Yet in many programs, the brontosaurus model is far from being extinct.

Leading Practices of High-Growth Companies*

Marketing, financial management, and planning are the practical side of how fast-growth entrepreneurs pursue opportunities; devise, manage, and orchestrate their financial strategies; build a team with collabora-

*Extracted from Donald L. Sexton and Forrest I. Seale, "Leading Practices of Fast Growth Entrepreneurs: Pathways to High Performance." Based upon data developed by the Ewing Marion Kauffman Foundation, Ernst & Young LLP and the Entrepreneur of the Year Institute. 1997. All rights reserved.

tive decision making; and plan with vision, clarity, and flexibility. Clearly, rapid growth is a different game, requiring an entrepreneurial mind-set and skills.

Growing Up Big

Stages of Growth Revisited

Managing and growing a high-potential small business is a different managerial game than sustaining an operation. Ventures in the high-growth stage face forces that tend to limit the creativity of the founders and team; that cause confusion and resentment over roles, responsibilities, and goals that call for specialization; that require operating mechanisms and controls and therefore erode collaboration. You will find this contrary to the entrepreneurial behavior you are used to. The reality is that structures, procedures, and patterns are fluid, and all members of the organization—not just the founder—will have to respond with entrepreneurial thinking.

The first three years before start-up are called the *research-and-development* (R&D) *stage*; the first three years, the *start-up stage*; years four through ten, the *early-growth stage*; the tenth year through the fifteenth or so, *maturity*; and after the fifteenth year, *stability*. Remember that these time estimates are approximate and will vary by industry and particular circumstances.

Various models depict the life cycle of a growing firm as a smooth curve with rapidly ascending sales and profits and a leveling off toward the peak before dipping toward decline. In truth, however, very few, if any, growing firms experience such smooth and linear phases of growth. By and large, if the actual growth curves of companies are plotted over ten years, the curves will look far more like the ups and downs of a roller-coaster ride than the smooth progressions usually depicted. Over the life of a typical growing firm, there are periods of jerks, bumps, hiccups, indigestion, and renewal interspersed with periods of smooth sailing. Sometimes there is continual upward progress through all this, but with others, there are periods where the firms seem near collapse or at least in considerable peril. Ed Marram, an entrepreneur and educator for twenty years, characterizes the five stages of a firm as Wonder, Blunder, Thunder, Plunder, and Asunder (see Exhibit 8.1). Wonder is the period that is filled with uncertainty about survival. Blunder is a growth stage when many firms stumble and fail. The Thunder stage occurs when growth is robust and the entrepreneur has built a solid management team. Cash flow is robust during Plunder, but in Asunder the firm needs to renew or it will decline.

Core Management Mode

As was noted earlier, changes in several critical variables determine just how frantic or easy transitions from one stage to the next will be. As a result, it is possible to make some generalizations about the main management challenges and transitions that will be encountered as the com-

Exhibit 8.1 Growth Stages

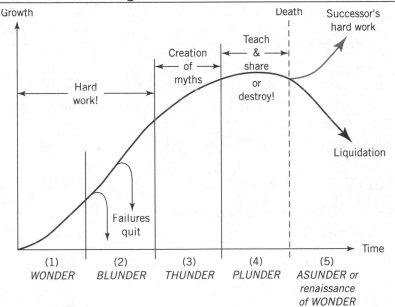

pany grows. The core management mode is influenced by the number of employees a firm has, which is in turn related to its dollar sales.*

Until sales reach approximately $5 million and employees number about twenty-five, the core management mode is one of *doing*. It becomes *managing* with between $5 million and $15 million in sales and twenty-five to seventy-five employees. When sales exceed $10 million and employees number over seventy-five, the core management mode is *managing managers*. Obviously, these revenue and employment figures are broad generalities. The number of people is a better indicator of the increasing complexity of the management task, and suggests a new wall to be scaled, rather than a precise point. Explosive sales per employee was one of the failed promises of the Internet, and to some extent the irrational dot-com valuations of the late 1990s were an anticipation of technology massively leveraging variable employee expense.

The central issue facing entrepreneurs in all sorts of businesses is this: as the size of the firm increases, the core management mode likewise changes, *from doing, to managing, to managing managers*. During each of the stages of growth of a firm, most firms will confront entrepreneurial crises, or hurdles. Here we consider by stage some indications of crisis.† As Exhibit 8.2 shows, for each fundamental driving force of entrepreneurship, there are a number of "signals" that crises are imminent. While the list is long, these are not the only indicators of crises new ventures can and most likely will see—only the most common. Of course, each of these signals does not necessarily indicate that particular crises will happen to every company at each stage—but when the signals are there, serious difficulties cannot be too far behind.

The Problem in Rate of Growth

Difficulties in anticipating these shifts by recognizing signals and developing management approaches are compounded by growth rate. The

*Harvey "Chet" Krentzman described this phenomenon to one of the authors many years ago. The principle still applies.

†The crises discussed here are the ones the authors consider particularly critical. Usually, failure to overcome even a few can seriously imperil a venture at a given stage. There are, however, many more, but a comprehensive treatment is outside the scope of this book.

Exhibit 8.2 Crises and Symptoms

Pre-Start-Up (Years −3 to −1)

Entrepreneurs
- **Focus.** Is the founder really an entrepreneur, bent on building a company, or an inventor, technical dilettante, or the like?
- **Selling.** Does the team have the necessary selling and closing skills to bring in the business and make the plan—on time?
- **Management.** Does the team have the necessary management skills and relevant experience, or is it overloaded in one or two areas (e.g., finance or technology)?
- **Ownership.** Have the critical decisions about ownership and equity splits been resolved, and are the members committed to these?

Opportunity
- **Focus.** Is the business really user, customer, and market driven (by a need), or is it driven by an invention or a desire to create?
- **Customers.** Have customers been identified with specific names, addresses, and phone numbers, and have purchase levels been estimated—or is the business still only at the concept stage?
- **Supply.** Are costs, margins, and lead times to acquire supplies, components, and key people known?
- **Strategy.** Is the entry plan a shotgun and cherry-picking strategy, or is it a rifle shot at a well-focused niche?

Resources
- **Resources.** Have the required capital resources been identified?
- **Cash.** Are the founders already out of cash (OOC) and their own resources?
- **Business plan.** Is there a business plan or is the team "hoofing it"?

Start-Up and Survival (Years 0–3)

Entrepreneurs
- **Leadership.** Has a top leader been accepted, or are founders vying for the decision role or insisting on equality in all decisions?
- **Goals.** Do the founders share and have compatible goals and work styles, or are these starting to conflict and diverge once the enterprise is under way and pressures mount?
- **Management.** Are the founders anticipating and preparing for a shift from doing to managing and letting go—of decisions and control—that will be required to make the plan on time?

Opportunity
- **Economics.** Are the economic benefits and payback to the customer actually being achieved and on time?
- **Strategy.** Is the company a one-product company with no encore in sight?
- **Competition.** Have previously unknown competitors or substitutes appeared in the marketplace?
- **Distribution.** Are there surprises and difficulties in actually achieving planned channels of distribution on time?

(continued)

Exhibit 8.2 Crises and Symptoms *(continued)*

Resources
- **Cash.** Is the company facing a cash crunch early as a result of not having a business plan (and a financial plan)? That is, is it facing a crunch because no one is asking: When will we run out of cash? Are the owners' pocketbooks exhausted?
- **Schedule.** Is the company experiencing serious deviation from projections and time estimates in the business plan? Is the company able to marshal resources according to plan and on time?

Early Growth (Years 4–10)

Entrepreneurs
- **Doing or managing.** Are the founders still just doing, or are they managing for results by a plan? Have the founders begun to delegate and let go of critical decisions, or do they maintain veto power over all significant decisions?
- **Focus.** Is the mind-set of the founders operational only, or is there some serious strategic thinking going on as well?

Opportunity
- **Market.** Are repeat sales and sales to new customers being achieved on time, according to plan, and because of interaction with customers, or are these coming from the engineering, R&D, or planning group? Is the company shifting to a marketing orientation without losing its killer instinct for closing sales?
- **Competition.** Are price and quality being blamed for loss of customers or for an inability to achieve targets in the sales plan, while customer service is rarely mentioned?
- **Economics.** Are gross margins beginning to erode?

Resources
- **Financial control.** Are accounting and information systems and control (purchasing orders, inventory, billing, collections, cost and profit analysis, cash management, etc.) keeping pace with growth and being there as needed?
- **Cash.** Is the company always out of cash—or nearly OOC—and is no one asking when it will run out or is sure why or what to do about it?
- **Contracts.** Has the company developed the outside networks (directors, contracts, etc.) it needs to continue growth?

Maturity (Years 10–15+)

Entrepreneurs
- **Goals.** Are the partners in conflict over control, goals, or underlying ethics or values?
- **Health.** Are there signs of instability in any founder's marriage, health, or emotions (i.e., are there extramarital affairs, drug and/or alcohol abuse, or fights and temper tantrums with partners or spouses)?
- **Teamwork.** Is there a sense of team building for a "greater purpose," with the founders now managing managers, or is there conflict over control of the company and disintegration?

Opportunity
- **Economics/competition.** Are the products and/or services that have gotten the company this far experiencing unforgiving economics as a result of perishability, competitor blind sides, new technology, or off-shore competition—and is there a plan to respond?
- **Product encore.** Has a major new product introduction been a failure?
- **Strategy.** Has the company continued to cherry-pick in fast growth markets, with a resulting lack of strategic definition (which opportunities to say no to)?

Resources
- **Cash.** Is the firm OOC again?
- **Development/information.** Has growth gotten out of control, with systems, training, and development of new managers failing to keep pace?
- **Financial control.** Have systems continued to lag behind sales?

Harvest/Stability (Years 15–20+)

Entrepreneurs
- **Succession/ownership.** Are there mechanisms in place to provide for management succession and the handling of very tricky ownership issues (especially family)?
- **Goals.** Have the partners' personal and financial goals and priorities begun to conflict and diverge? Are any of the founders simply bored or burned out, and are they seeking a change of view and activities?
- **Entrepreneurial passion.** Has there been an erosion of the passion for creating value through the recognition and pursuit of opportunity? Are turf building, acquiring status and power symbols, and gaining control favored?

Opportunity
- **Strategy.** Is there a spirit of innovation and renewal in the firm (e.g., a goal that half the company's sales come from products or services less than five years old), or has lethargy set in?
- **Economics.** Have the core economics and durability of the opportunity eroded so far that profitability and return on investment are nearly as low as that for the Fortune 500?

Resources
- **Cash.** Has OOC been solved by increasing bank debt and leverage because the founders do not want—or cannot agree—to give up equity?
- **Accounting.** Have accounting and legal issues, especially their relevance for wealth building and estate and tax planning, been anticipated and addressed? Has a harvest concept been part of the long-range planning process?

faster the rate of growth, the greater the potential for difficulty; this is because of the various pressures, chaos, confusion, and loss of control. It is not an exaggeration to say that these pressures and demands increase geometrically, rather than in a linear way.

Growth rates affect all aspects of a business. Thus, as sales increase, as more people are hired, and as inventory increases, sales outpace manufacturing capacity. Facilities are then increased, people are moved between buildings, accounting systems and controls cannot keep up, and so on. The cash burn rate accelerates. As such acceleration continues, learning curves do the same. Worst of all, cash collections lag behind, as shown in Exhibit 8.3.

Distinctive issues caused by rapid growth were considered at seminars at Babson College with the founders and presidents of rapidly growing companies—companies with sales of at least $1 million and growing in excess of 30 percent per year.* These founders and presidents pointed to the following concerns:

- **Opportunity overload.** Rather than lacking enough sales or new market opportunities (a classic concern in mature companies), these firms faced an abundance. Choosing from among these was a problem.
- **Abundance of capital.** While most stable or established smaller or medium-sized firms often have difficulties obtaining equity and debt financing, most of the rapidly growing firms were not constrained by this. The problem was, rather, how to evaluate investors as "partners" and the terms of the deals with which they were presented.
- **Misalignment of cash burn and collection rates.** These firms all pointed to problems of cash burn rates racing ahead of collections. They found that unless effective integrated accounting, inventory, purchasing, shipping, and invoicing systems and controls are in place, this misalignment can lead to chaos and collapse. One firm, for example, had tripled its sales in three years from $5 million to $16 million. Suddenly, its president resigned, insisting that, with the systems

*These seminars were held at Babson College near Boston between 1985 and 1999. A good number of the firms represented had sales over $1 million, and many were growing at greater than 100 percent per year.

Exhibit 8.3 Spend Rate/Orders/Collection Leads and Lags

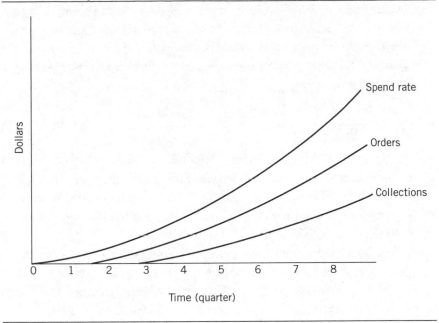

that were in place, the company would be able to grow to $100 million. However, the computer system was disastrously inadequate, which compounded other management weaknesses. The generation of any believable financial and accounting information that could be relied upon was not possible for many months. Losses of more than $1 million annually mounted, and the company's lenders panicked. To make matters worse, the auditors failed to stay on top of the situation until it was too late, and they were replaced. While the company has survived, it has had to restructure its business and has shrunk to $6 million in sales, to pay off bank debt and to avoid bankruptcy. Fortunately, it is in the process of recovering.

- **Decision making.** Many of the firms succeeded because they executed functional day-to-day and week-to-week decisions, rather than strategizing. Strategy had to take a backseat. Many of the representatives of these firms argued that in conditions of rapid growth, strategy was only about 10 percent of the story.

- **Expanding facilities and space . . . and surprises.** Expansion of space or facilities is a problem and one of the most disrupting events during the early explosive growth of a company. Managers of many of these firms were not prepared for the surprises, delays, organizational difficulties, and system interruptions that are spawned by such expansion.

Industry Turbulence

The problems just discussed are compounded by the amount of industry turbulence surrounding the venture. Firms with higher growth rates are usually found in industries that are also developing rapidly. In addition, there are often many new entrants, both with competing products or services and with substitutes.

The effects are many. Often, prices fluctuate. The turbulence in the semiconductor industry in the 1980s is a good example. From June 1984 to June 1985, the price to original equipment manufacturers (OEMs) of 64K memory chips fell from $2.50 each to 50 cents. The price to OEMs of 256K chips fell from $15 to $3. The same devastating industry effect manifested in the years 2000–2002 when cellular airtime pricing plunged by more than 50 percent. The disruption this caused in marketing and sales projections, in financial planning and cash forecasting, and the like, for firms in theses industries can be imagined. Often, too, there are rapid shifts in cost and experience curves. The consequences of missed steps in growing businesses are profound.

The Importance of Culture and Organizational Climate

Six Dimensions

The organizational culture and climate, either of a new venture or of an existing organization, are critical in how well the organization will deal with growth. A number of studies of performance in large business organizations that used the concept of organizational climate (i.e., the perceptions of people about the kind of place it is to work in) have led to two general conclusions. First, the climate of an organization can significantly impact performance. Further, climate is created both by the expectations people bring to the organization and the practices and attitudes of the key managers.

The climate notion has relevance for new ventures as well as for entrepreneurial efforts in large organizations. An entrepreneur's style and priorities—particularly, how he or she manages tasks and people— is well known by the people being managed and affects performance. Roger Enrico, former chair of Pepsi, describes the critical factors for growth as setting high-performance standards by developing short-run objectives that do not sacrifice long-run results, providing responsive personal leadership, encouraging individual initiative, helping others to succeed, and developing individual networks for success.

Evidence suggests that superior teams operate differently in terms of setting priorities, in resolving leadership issues, in what and how roles are performed by team members, in attitudes toward listening and participation, and in dealing with disagreements. Further, evidence suggests that specific approaches to management can impact the climate of a growing organization. For example, gains *from* the motivation, commitment, and teamwork, which are anchored in a consensus approach to management, while not immediately apparent, are striking later on. At that time there is swiftness and decisiveness in actions and in follow-through, since the negotiating, compromising, and accepting of priorities are history. Also, new disagreements that emerge generally do not bring progress to a halt, since there is both high clarity and broad acceptance of overall goals and underlying priorities. Without this consensus, each new problem or disagreement often necessitates a time-consuming and painful confrontation and renegotiation, simply because it was not done initially.

Organizational climate can be described along six basic dimensions:

- **Clarity:** the degree of organizational clarity in terms of being well organized, concise, and efficient in the way that tasks, procedures, and assignments are made and accomplished
- **Standards:** the degree to which management expects and puts pressure on employees for high standards and excellent performance
- **Commitment:** the extent to which employees feel committed to the goals and objectives of the organization

- **Responsibility:** the extent to which members of the organization feel responsibility for accomplishing their goals without being constantly monitored and second-guessed
- **Recognition:** the extent to which employees feel they are recognized and rewarded (nonmonetarily) for a job well done, instead of only being punished for mistakes or errors
- **Esprit de corps:** the extent to which employees feel a sense of cohesion and team spirit, of working well together

Approaches to Management

In achieving the entrepreneurial culture and climate described above, certain approaches to management are common across core management modes.

Leadership. No single leadership pattern seems to characterize successful ventures. Leadership may be shared, or informal, or a natural leader may guide a task. Common, however, is the pattern whereby a manager defines and gains agreements on who has what responsibility and authority and who works with whom. Roles, tasks, responsibilities, accountabilities, and appropriate approvals are defined.

There is no competition for leadership in these organizations: leadership is based on expertise, not authority. Emphasis is placed on performing task-oriented roles, but someone invariably provides for "maintenance" and group cohesion by good humor and wit. Further, the leader does not force his or her own solution on the team or exclude the involvement of potential resources. Instead, the leader understands the relationships among tasks and between the leader and his or her followers and is able to lead in those situations where it is appropriate, including dynamically managing the activities of others through directions and suggestions.

This approach is in direct contrast to the commune approach, where two to four entrepreneurs, usually friends or work acquaintances, leave unanswered such questions as who is in charge, who makes the final decisions, and how real differences of opinion are resolved. While some overlapping of roles and a sharing in and negotiating of decisions are desirable in a new venture, too much looseness is debilitating. This approach also diverges from situations where a self-appointed leader takes over, where there is competition for leadership, or where one task takes precedence over other tasks.

Consensus Building. Leaders of most successful new ventures define authority and responsibility in a way that builds motivation and commitment to cross-departmental and corporate goals. Using a consensus approach to management requires managing and working with peers and with the subordinates of others (or with superiors) outside formal chains of command, while balancing multiple viewpoints and demands.

In the consensus approach, the manager is seen as willing to relinquish his or her priorities and power in the interests of an overall goal, and the appropriate people are included in setting cross-functional or cross-departmental goals and in making decisions. Participation and listening are emphasized.

In addition, the most effective managers are committed to dealing with and resolving problems by seeking a reconciliation of viewpoints, rather than emphasizing differences, and by blending ideas, rather than playing the role of hard-nosed negotiator or devil's advocate to force their own solution. There is open confrontation and a willingness to talk out differences, assumptions, reasons, and inferences. Logic and reason tend to prevail, and there is a willingness to change opinions based on consensus.

Communication. The most effective managers share information and are willing to alter individual views. Listening and participation are facilitated by such methods as circular seating arrangements, few interruptions or side conversations, and calm discussion versus many interruptions, loud or separate conversations, and so forth, in meetings.

Encouragement. Successful managers build confidence by encouraging innovation and calculated risk taking, rather than by punishing or criticizing what is less than perfect, and by expecting and encouraging others to find and correct their own errors and to solve their own problems. Their peers and others perceive them as accessible and willing to help when needed, and they provide the necessary resources to enable others to do the job. When it is appropriate, they go to bat for their peers and subordinates, even when they know they cannot always win. Further, differences are recognized and performance is rewarded.

Trust. The most effective managers are perceived as trustworthy and straightforward. They do what they say they are going to do; they are not the corporate rumor carriers; they are open and spontaneous, rather than guarded and cautious with each word; and they are perceived as being honest and direct. They have a reputation of getting results and are known as the creative problem solvers who have a knack for blending and balancing multiple views and demands.

Development. Effective managers have a reputation for developing human capital (i.e., they groom and grow other effective managers by their example and their mentoring). David Bradford and Allan Cohen[1] distinguish between the heroic manager, whose need to be in control may actually stifle cooperation, and the postheroic manager, a developer who actually brings about excellence in organizations by developing entrepreneurial middle management. If a company puts off developing middle management until they make the growth decision, the organization may come unraveled when the plan is executed. Linking a plan to grow human capital at the middle management and the supervisory levels with the business strategy is an essential first step.

Entrepreneurial Management for the Twenty-First Century: Three Breakthroughs

Three extraordinary companies have been built or revolutionized since 1980: JetBlue; Springfield Remanufacturing Corporation of Springfield, Missouri; and Johnsonville Sausage of Sheboygan, Wisconsin. Independently and unbeknownst to one another, these companies created what we describe as "high-standard, perpetual-learning cultures," which create and foster a "chain of greatness." The lessons from these three great companies provide a blueprint for entrepreneurial management in the twenty-first century. They set the standard and provide a tangible vision of what is possible. Not surprisingly, the most exciting, faster-growing, and profitable companies in America today have striking similarities to these firms.

David Neeleman and JetBlue

U.S. airlines has been considered one of the stoogiest, large-company-dominated industries ever. It requires very high fixed costs; its largest variable cost (at 25 percent) is outside the business's control; profits are low or even negative; and it is dominated by the highest-paid union in business. How could any start-up begin to think it could raise money, get off the ground, and succeed in 1999? David Neeleman, and his venture capital lead backer, Michael Lazarus of Weston-Presidio Partners, epitomize the entrepreneurial thinking and process, creative strategies, and breakthrough management approaches that we have highlighted in this book. And they are revolutionizing the airline industry in ways none of the established players ever imagined: fly people where they want to go rather than where you want to build hubs; make everything electronic—from tickets to flight and maintenance logs to all record keeping and documentation (Neeleman invented the first electronic ticket); customize and create highly flexible and the highest paid jobs in the industry; build a great team and don't insist that they all work at one location (the vice president of human resources, Ann Rhoades, lives and works out of Santa Fe, New Mexico, while JetBlue's headquarters is on Long Island); and create and live by a culture of five core values: (1) safety, (2) caring, (3) integrity, (4) fun, and (5) passion. The company in its first year (2000) operated ten Airbus 320s and employed nearly 1,000 people. By 2004, it expected to have 5,000 people on its payroll. JetBlue has had an initial public offering of stock and has a market capitalization over $8 billion. This is an industry with a lot of technology-based innovation but surprisingly little entrepreneurial thinking, with the exception of People Express and Southwest Airlines. JetBlue is a stunning reminder of how the entrepreneurial revolution is driven by people and leadership.

Jack Stack and Springfield Remanufacturing Corporation

The truly remarkable sage of this revolution in management is Jack Stack. His book *The Great Game of Business* is a must-read for any entrepreneur. In 1983, Stack and a dozen colleagues acquired a tractor engine remanufacturing plant from the failing International Harvester Corporation. With an 89-to-1 debt-to-equity ratio and 21 percent interest, they acquired the company for 10 cents a share. In 2003, the company's shares were valued near $30 for the employee stock option plan (ESOP), and the company had completely turned around with sales exceeding $160 million. What had happened?

Jack Stack created and implemented some management approaches and values that deviated radically from the top-down, hierarchical, custodial management commonly found in large manufacturing enterprises. At the heart of his leadership was creating a vision called the Big Picture:

> *Think and act like owners, be the best we can be, and be perpetual learners. Build teamwork as the key by learning from each other, open the books to everyone, and educate everyone so they can become responsible and accountable for the numbers, both short- and long-term.*

How can the Big Picture be implemented? Stack puts it this way:

> *We try to take ignorance out of the workplace and force people to get involved, not with threats and intimidation but with education. In the process, we are trying to close the biggest gaps in American business— the gap between workers and managers. We're developing a system that allows everyone to get together and work toward the same goals. To do that, you have to knock down the barriers that separate people that keep people from coming together as a team.*[2]

At Springfield Remanufacturing Corporation, everyone learns to read and interpret all the financial statements, including an income statement, balance sheet, and cash flow, and how his or her job affects each line item. This open-book management style is linked with pushing responsibility downward and outward, and to understanding both wealth creation (i.e., shareholder value) and wealth sharing through short-term bonuses and long-term equity participation. Jack describes the value of this approach thus: "The payoff comes from getting the people who create the numbers to understand the numbers. When that happens, the communication between the bottom and the top of the organization is just phenomenal."[3] The results he has achieved in ten years are nothing short of astounding. What is more amazing is that he has found the time to share this approach with others. To date, over 150 companies have participated in seminars that have enabled them to adopt his approach.

Ralph Stayer and Johnsonville Sausage Company[4]

In 1975, Johnsonville Sausage was a small company with about $5 million in sales and a fairly traditional, hierarchical, and somewhat custodial management. In just a few years, Ralph Stayer, the owner's son, radically transformed the company, with a management revolution whose values, culture, and philosophy are very similar to the principles of Jack Stack and David Neeleman.

Remarkably, by 1980 the company had reached $15 million in sales; by 1985, $50 million; and by 1990, $150 million. At the heart of the changes he created was the concept of a *total learning culture*: everyone is a learner, seeking to improve constantly, finding better ways. High performance standards, accompanied by an investment in training and performance measures that made it possible to reward fairly both short- and long-term results, were critical to the transition. Responsibility and accountability was spread downward and outward. For example, instead of forwarding complaint letters to the marketing department, where they are filed and the standard response is sent, they go directly to the frontline sausage stuffer responsible for the product's taste. They are the ones who respond to customer complaints now. Another example is the interviewing, hiring, and training process for new people. A newly hired woman pointed out numerous shortcomings with the existing process and proposed ways to improve it. As a result, the entire responsibility was shifted from the traditional human resources/personnel group to the frontline, with superb results.

As one would guess, such radical changes do not come easily. After all, how are such changes ever initiated in the first place? Consider Ralph's insight:

> *In 1980, I began looking for a recipe for change. I started by searching for a book that would tell me how to get people to care about their jobs and their company. Not surprisingly, the search was fruitless. No one could tell me how to wake up my own workforce; I would have to figure it out for myself. . . . The most important question any manager can ask is: "In the best of all possible worlds what would I really want to happen?"*[5]

Even having taken such a giant leap, Ralph was ready to take the next, equally perilous steps:

> *Acting on instinct, I ordered a change. "From now on," I announced to my management team, "you're all responsible for making your own decisions." . . . I went from authoritarian control to authoritarian abdication. No one had asked for more responsibility; I had forced it down their throats.*[6]

Further insight into just how challenging it is to transform a company like Johnsonville Sausage is revealed in another Stayer quote:

> *I spent those two years pursuing another mirage as well—detailed strategic and tactical plans that would realize my goals of Johnsonville as the world's greatest sausage maker. We tried to plan organizational structure two to three years before it would be needed. . . . Later I realized that these structural changes had to grow from day-to-day working realities; no one could dictate them from above, and certainly not in advance.*[7]

Exhibit 8.4 summarizes the key steps in the transformation of Johnsonville Sausage over several years. Such a picture undoubtedly oversimplifies the process and understates the extraordinary commitment and effort required to pull it off, but it does show how the central elements weave together.

The Chain of Greatness

As we reflect on these three great companies, we can see that there is clearly a pattern here, with some common denominators in both the ingredients and the process. This chain of greatness becomes reinforcing and perpetuating (see Exhibit 8.5). Leadership that instills across the company a vision of greatness and an owner's mentality is a common beginning. A philosophy of perpetual learning throughout the organization accompanied by high standards of performance is key to the value-creating entrepreneurial cultures at the three firms. A culture that teaches and rewards teamwork, improvement, and respect for one another provides the oil and glue to make things work. Finally, a fair

Exhibit 8.4   Critical Aspects of the Johnsonville Sausage Company's Transition

1. It started at the top: Ralph Stayer recognized that he was the heart of the problem and recognized the need to change—the most difficult step.
2. Vision was anchored in human resource management and in a particular idea of the company's culture:
   - continuous learning organization
   - team concept—change players
   - new model of jobs (Ralph Stayer's role and decision making)
   - performance- and results-based compensation and rewards
3. Stayer decided to push responsibility and accountability downward to the frontline decision makers:
   - frontliners are closest to the customer and the problem
   - define the whole task
   - invest in training and selection
   - job criteria and feedback = development tool
4. Controls and mechanisms make it work:
   - measure performance—not behavior, activities, and the like
   - emphasize learning and development, not allocation of blame
   - customize to you and the company
   - decentralize and minimize staff

and generous short- and long-term reward system, as well as the necessary education to make sure that everyone knows and can use the numbers, creates a mechanism for sharing the wealth with those who contributed to it. The results speak for themselves: extraordinary levels of personal, professional, and financial achievement.

Conclusion

Most successful small business owners have nimble and responsive organizations. The demands of rapid growth will stress those organizations and challenge the entrepreneur to continually reinvent the management structure. The entrepreneurial organization today is flatter, faster, more

Exhibit 8.5 The Chain of Greatness

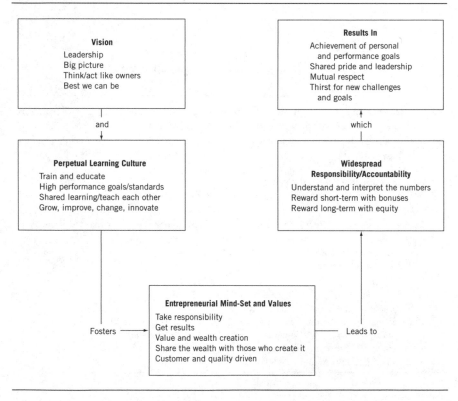

flexible and responsive, and copes readily with ambiguity and change. It is the opposite of the hierarchical, layered management, and the more-is-better syndrome prevalent in brontosaurus capitalism. For you to distinguish your company as a high-value firm, you must be a leader in the entrepreneurial practices of marketing, finance, management, and planning. And you will be challenged as you grow! Remember, you will likely go through the Wonder, Blunder, Thunder, Plunder, and Asunder (or Wonder again) stages. Establishing or maintaining a culture and climate conducive to entrepreneurship is a core task for the venture. In the process of growing your company you might create the kind of "chain of greatness" that people like David Neeleman, Jack Stack, and Ralph Stayer produced.

Notes

1. Allan R. Cohen and David L. Bradford, *Influence Without Authority* (Hoboken, NJ: John Wiley and Sons, Inc., 1991).

2. Jack Stack, *The Great Game of Business* (New York: Currency/Doubleday Books, 1991), p. 5.

3. Ibid., p. 93.

4. For an excellent discussion of this transformation, see "The Johnsonville Sausage Company," HBS Case 9-387-103, revised December 20, 1993. Copyright © 1986 by the President and Fellows of Harvard College. See also Ralph Stayer, "How I Learned to Let My Workers Lead," *Harvard Business Review*, Nov.–Dec. 1990. Copyright © 1990 by the President and Fellows of Harvard College.

5. Stayer, "How I Learned to Let My Workers Lead," p. 1.

6. Ibid., pp. 3–4.

7. Ibid., p. 4.

CHAPTER 9

THE HARVEST
AND BEYOND

"And don't forget: shrouds have no pockets."
— THE LATE SIDNEY RABB, CHAIRMAN EMERITUS,
STOP & SHOP, BOSTON

A Journey, Not a Destination

A common sentiment among successful entrepreneurs is that it is the challenge and exhilaration of the journey that gives them the greatest kick. Henry Ford, a driven entrepreneur, said, "If money is your hope for independence you will never have it. The only real security that a man will have in this world is a reserve of knowledge, experience, and ability." It is the thrill of the chase that counts.

These entrepreneurs also talk of the venture's incredibly insatiable appetite for not only cash but also time, attention, and energy. Some say it is an addiction. Most say it is far more demanding and difficult than they ever imagined. Most, however, plan not to retire and would do it again, usually sooner. What's more, they also say it is more fun and satisfying than any other career they have had.

For the vast majority of entrepreneurs it takes ten, fifteen, even twenty years or more to build a significant net worth. According to the popular press and government statistics, there are more millionaires than ever in America. In 2002, it was estimated that as many as 3.5 million persons in the United States (or nearly 3 percent of the working population) would be millionaires—their net worth exceeding $1 million. While these numbers may be true, a million dollars, sadly, is not really all that much money today as a result of inflation; and while lottery and sweepstakes winners become instant millionaires, entrepreneurs do not.

The Journey Can Be Addictive

Considering the total immersion required—the huge workload, the many sacrifices for a family, and the burnout often experienced by entrepreneurs during the journey—maintaining the energy, enthusiasm, and drive to get across the finish line, to achieve a harvest, may be exceptionally difficult. Terri Lonier, founder of the Solo Entrepreneur's Network, relates that many entrepreneurs are torn between staying small and "controlling" their business or growing and losing control. Yet they sometimes feel trapped by the business. Most have never planned a harvest strategy. It is imperative that entrepreneurs think about the endgame at the beginning of the journey. Unless we understand what success means to us in advance, we may not know if we have achieved it. We very well may be trapped!

The opening quote of the chapter is a sobering reminder that you can't take your money with you. Its message is clear: unless an entrepreneur enjoys the journey and thinks it is worthwhile, he or she may end up on the wrong train, going to the wrong destination.

First Build a Great Company

One of the simplest, but most difficult, principles for nonentrepreneurs to grasp is that wealth and liquidity are results—not causes—of building a great company. They fail to recognize the difference between making money and spending money. Most successful entrepreneurs possess a clear understanding of this distinction; they are driven and fulfilled by growing their company. They know the payoff will take care of itself if they concentrate on the money-making part of the process.

Create Harvest Options

Here is yet another great paradox in the entrepreneurial process: build a great company and plan to harvest. This apparent contradiction is difficult to reconcile, especially among entrepreneurs with several generations in a family-owned enterprise. Perhaps a better way to frame this apparent contradiction is to keep harvest options open and to think of harvesting as a vehicle for reducing risk and for creating future entrepreneurial choices and options—not simply selling the business and heading for the golf course or the beach, although these options may appeal to a few entrepreneurs.

So many entrepreneurs erroneously assume that the business will go on forever. By stubbornly and steadfastly refusing to explore harvest options and exiting as a natural part of the entrepreneurial process, owners may actually *increase* their overall risk and deprive themselves of future options. Innumerable examples exist whereby entrepreneurs sold or merged their companies and then went on to acquire or to start another company and pursued new dreams:

- Robin Wolaner founded *Parenting* magazine in the mid-1980s and sold it to Time-Life.[1] Wolaner then joined Time and built a highly successful career there, and in July of 1992, she became the head of Time's Sunset Publishing Corporation.[2]
- Securities Online was launched by Gary and George Muller while Gary was still an MBA student in the early 1990s. That company rapidly became quite successful and was sold in early 2000 for over $50 million. Gary made a significant capital gain but stayed with the new owners as president. George created ColorKinetics, Inc., in Boston. That company, by early 2004, had raised nearly $30 million of venture capital and will likely exceed $40 million in sales in 2004 as the leading firm in LED lighting technology. The company was

in the registration process for an IPO in spring 2004. Harvest is a mechanism for doing *more* business.

- Craig Benson founded Cabletron in the 1980s, and it flourished. Eventually he brought in a new CEO and became involved as a trustee of Babson College, and then began teaching entrepreneurship classes with a focus on information technology and the Internet. Now, as governor of New Hampshire, he has found another way to give back to society and to pursue new dreams.

- After creating and building the ninth-largest pharmaceutical company in the United States, Marion Labs, Ewing Marion Kauffman led an extraordinary life as philanthropist and sportsman. His Kauffman Foundation and its Center for Entrepreneurial Leadership have become the first and premier foundation in the nation dedicated to accelerating entrepreneurship in America. He brought major-league baseball to Kansas City and made sure it would stay there by gifting the Royals to the city and stipulating that the team not relocate when it was sold. The $75 million proceeds of the sale were also donated to charitable causes in Kansas City.

- Jeff Parker built and sold two companies, including Technical Data Corporation,[3] by the time he was forty. His substantial gain from these ventures has led to an entire new career as a private investor who works closely with young entrepreneurs to help them build their companies.

These are a tiny representation of the tens of thousands of entrepreneurs that build on their platforms of entrepreneurial success to pursue highly meaningful lives in philanthropy, public service, and community leadership roles. By realizing a harvest, such options become possible, yet the vast majority of entrepreneurs make these contributions to society while continuing to build their companies. This is one of the best-kept secrets in American culture: the public has very little awareness and appreciation of just how much entrepreneurs give back to their communities through their time, their leadership, and their money. One could fill a book with numerous other examples. The entrepreneurial process is endless.

A Harvest Goal

Having a harvest goal and crafting a strategy to achieve it are certainly what separate successful entrepreneurs from the rest of the pack. Indeed, we have found that small business owners who have a well-planned harvest option tend to be more successful because they are driven by specific goals. Many entrepreneurs seek only to create a job and a living for themselves. But it is quite another thing to grow a business that creates a living for many others, including employees and investors, by creating value—value that can result in a capital gain.

Setting a harvest goal achieves many purposes, not the least of which is helping an entrepreneur get after-tax cash out of an enterprise and enhancing substantially his or her net worth. Such a goal also can create high standards and a serious commitment to excellence over the course of developing the business. It can provide, in addition, a motivating force and a strategic focus that does not sacrifice customers, employees, and value-added products and services just to maximize quarterly earnings.

There are other good reasons as well. Building a business, whether it is small or large, is hard work. Indeed, it may be easier to run a growing business. Growing businesses attract better talent and smarter money, because teams and investors believe there is an endgame that will benefit them and not just the owner. The workload is shared and the stress is spread across a broader base

Also, within the process of harvest, the seeds of renewal and reinvestment are sown. Harvest brings in new management with new ideas that may help the company achieve the next level of success. The cash that the entrepreneur and other team members receive provides fuel for new ventures and philanthropy. Likewise, investors use their proceeds to make new investments in different companies. Such a recycling of entrepreneurial talent and capital is at the very heart of our system of private responsibility for economic renewal and individual initiative. Entrepreneurial companies organize and manage for the long haul in ways to perpetuate the opportunity creation and recognition process and thereby to ensure the process of economic regeneration, innovation, and renewal.

Thus, a harvest goal is not just that of selling and leaving the company. Rather, it is a long-term goal to add real value to a business.

Crafting a Harvest Strategy: Timing Is Vital

Consistently, entrepreneurs avoid thinking about harvest issues. Only 15 percent of them have a formal written strategy for harvest in their business plans, and just 5 percent have a formal harvest plan written after the business plan.[4] But companies that consider growth have a greater propensity to think about and achieve a successful harvest.[5] The companies that do not plan growth avoid harvest plans: when a company is first launched, then struggles for survival, and finally begins its ascent, usually the furthest thing from its founder's mind is selling out. Selling is often viewed by the entrepreneur as the equivalent to complete abandonment of his or her very own "baby."

Thus, time and again, a founder does not consider selling out until terror, in the form of the possibility of losing the whole company, is experienced. Usually, this possibility comes unexpectedly: new technology threatens to leapfrog the current product line, a large competitor suddenly appears in a small market, or a major account is lost. A sense of panic then grips the founders and shareholders of the closely held firm, and the company is suddenly for sale—for sale at the wrong time, for the wrong reasons, and thus for the wrong price. Selling at the right time, willingly, involves discovering a strategic window, one of the many strategic windows that entrepreneurs must look for.

Many entrepreneurs find that a harvest strategy is a nonissue until something begins to sprout, and again there is a vast distance between expanding the existing revenue stream of an ongoing business and launching from ground zero. Most entrepreneurs agree that securing customers and generating continuing sales revenue are much harder and take much longer than even they could have imagined. Further, the ease with which those revenue estimates can be cast and manipulated on a spreadsheet belies the time and effort necessary to turn those projections into cash.

At some point, with a higher potential venture, it becomes possible to realize the harvest. In terms of the strategic window, it is wiser to sell when it is opening than when it is closing. Bernard Baruch's wisdom is as good as it gets on this matter. He has said, "I made all my money by selling too early." If the window is missed, disaster can strike.

A window of opportunity is not unlike an economic cycle. We've seen many booms and busts. Following a change in federal tax law in 1986 and the stock-market crash of 1987, there was a major softening of the real estate market in 1988. This very same pattern happened again in 2000–2002 after the dot-com bubble burst. The NASDAQ began to crash from its high of over 5,000 and had not even reached 2,000 by fall of 2003. California's Silicon Valley was particularly hard hit by the rapid downturn. Technology and Internet entrepreneurs who had exercised their stock options when their company's stock was soaring in the range of $80 to $100, or even $150, per share, on the hope that such escalation would continue for a long time, faced a rude awakening. As the stock plummeted to single-digit prices, they still faced a huge capital gain tax on the difference between the cost of their options and the price at which their stock was acquired. In one community of over two thousand homes with the lowest price around $1 million, only three or four were on the market in January 2001. By the middle of 2001, nearly sixty such homes were up for sale. Nationwide in 2001, the sale of homes priced above $1 million dropped 25 percent.

Shaping a harvest strategy is an enormously complicated and difficult area. Thus, work cannot begin too early. In 2001 and 2002, many major companies declared bankruptcy in the wake of the dot-com and stock-market crash, including luminaries such an Enron, Kmart, and Global Crossing, and dozens of lesser-known telecommunications and networking-related companies. This is one history lesson that seems to repeat itself. While building a company is the ultimate goal, failure to preserve the harvest option—and utilize it when it is available—can be deadly.

In shaping a harvest strategy, some guidelines and cautions can help:

- **Patience.** As has been shown, several years are required to build most successful companies; therefore, patience can be invaluable. A harvest strategy is more sensible if it allows for a time frame of at least three to five years and as many as seven to ten.

- **Mental toughness.** It takes a textured understanding of your industry and company to recognize the difference between a short-term problem and a real downturn. Don't panic as a result of precipitate events. Selling under duress is usually the worst of all worlds.

- **Realistic valuation.** If impatience is the enemy of an attractive harvest, then greed is its executioner. For example, an excellent, small firm in New England, which was nearly eighty years old and run by the third generation of a line of successful family leaders, had attracted a number of prospective buyers and obtained a bona fide offer for over $25 million. The owners, however, convinced themselves that this "great little company" was worth considerably more, and they held out. Before long, there were no buyers, and market circumstances changed unfavorably. In addition, interest rates skyrocketed. Soon thereafter, the company collapsed financially, ending up in bankruptcy.

- **Outside advice.** It is difficult but worthwhile to find an advisor who can help craft a harvest strategy while the business is growing and, at the same time, maintain objectivity about its value and have the patience and skill to maximize it. A major problem seems to be that people who sell businesses, such as investment bankers or business brokers, are performing the same economic role and function as real estate brokers; in essence, their incentive is their commissions during a quite short time frame, usually a matter of months. However, an advisor who works with a lead entrepreneur for as much as five years or more can help shape and implement a strategy for the whole business so that it is positioned to spot and respond to harvest opportunities when they appear.

Harvest Options

There are seven principal avenues by which a company can realize a harvest from the value it has created. Described below, these most commonly seem to occur in the order in which they are listed. No attempt is made here to elaborate on the brief descriptions, since entire books are written on each option, including their legal, tax, and accounting intricacies.

Capital Cow

A "capital cow" is to the entrepreneur what a "cash cow" is to a large corporation. In essence, the high-margin profitable venture (the cow) throws off more cash for personal use (the milk) than most entrepreneurs have the time, opportunity, or inclination for spending it. The result is a capital-rich and cash-rich company with enormous capacity for debt and reinvestment. Take, for instance, some of the largest franchisees of Dunkin' Donuts. With ten or more mature restaurants there is usually enough free cash flow to sustain a very comfortable lifestyle and build one or two new restaurants every year! Many franchisees diversify by owning the real estate as well as the business, providing the opportunity for many years of personal cash flow even after they sell the business.

Employee Stock Ownership Plan

Employee stock ownership plans (ESOPs) have become very popular among closely held companies as a valuation mechanism for stock for which there is no formal market. They are also vehicles through which founders can realize some liquidity from their stock by sales to the plan and other employees. And since an ESOP usually creates widespread ownership of stock among employees, it is viewed as a positive motivational device as well. A leveraged ESOP borrows money from the company or another financial institution to buy the company's stock, whether all at once or in parts. The entrepreneur may or may not exit the company, but in either case he or she gets a large amount of money—in essence, the annualized stream of free cash flow in one or a few payments.

ESOPs were initially created to provide for the retirement benefits of a firm's employees. However, about half of all ESOPs are used to create a market for the shares of current owners wishing to harvest.

Where most retirement plans limit the amount of stock in any one company the plan can own, an ESOP is designed to allow employees to invest primarily in the firm's stock. The U.S. government encourages this by providing significant tax advantages for ESOPs. ESOPs can be either leveraged or unleveraged. In an unleveraged ESOP, the company makes an annual contribution to the ESOP for the employees' retirement. The ESOP then uses the money to purchase shares of the company. An unleveraged ESOP usually provides a slower harvest for the entrepreneur.

Also, an ESOP covers all employees and the company has to disclose a great deal of confidential information. And the government changes the rules for ESOPs all the time. Always be sure to check the current rules and take financial advice from the appropriate legal and financial professionals.

Management Buyout

Another avenue, called a management buyout (MBO), is one by which a founder can realize a gain from a business by selling it to existing partners or to other key managers in the business. If the business has both assets and a healthy cash flow, the financing can be arranged via banks, insurance companies, and financial institutions that do leveraged buyouts (LBOs) and MBOs. Even if assets are thin, a healthy cash flow that can service the debt to fund the purchase price can convince lenders to do the MBO.

Usually, the problem is that the managers who want to buy out the owners and remain to run the company lack the capital to do so. Unless the buyer has the cash up front—and this is rarely the case—such a sale can be very fragile, and full realization of a gain is questionable. MBOs typically require the seller to take a limited amount of cash up front and a note for the balance of the purchase price over several years. If the purchase price is linked to the future profitability of the business, the seller is totally dependent on the ability and integrity of the buyer. Further, the management, under such an arrangement, can lower the price by growing the business as fast as possible, spending on new products and people, and showing very little profit along the way. In these cases, it is often seen that after the marginally profitable business is sold at a bargain price, it is well positioned with excellent earnings in the next two or three years. Clearly, the seller will end up on the short end of this type of deal.

Management buyouts are typically classified as "financial engineering" strategies. In an MBO a small group of senior managers within the firm will attempt to purchase the company from the existing shareholders. These transactions often include some form of leveraged financing, but the team may be able to raise the necessary funds from their own resources. So, like 1980s takeover artists Carl Icahn and T. Boone Pickens, management will seek some equity and usually heavy debt financing to consummate these deals. A heavily leveraged deal puts pressure on the company to increase free cash flow for debt service.

A leveraged buyout or management buyout (LBO/MBO) strategy can make sense when the acquirer uses the base income stream to secure debt and infuses significant equity capital into the company. That is a very difficult task for an acquirer if there is an ongoing need to funnel free cash flow into growth plans. Another tactic of the LBO/MBO is to sell off assets of the company to reduce debt. This usually occurs where there are parts of the business that are not relevant for the new owner. For some people an LBO/MBO signals a retreat from growth.

Merger, Acquisition, and Strategic Alliance

Why would someone give you a lot of money for your company? Because they believe they can make more money than you did. The sale of one company to another, or the merger of two companies, occurs because the players believe the combined entity will better create wealth for the owners. Merging with another firm is still another way for a founder to realize a gain. For example, David Townsend owned a tractor-trailer sales, repair, and parts company. Faced with more and more competition, he believed only larger firms would survive. Townsend, therefore, positioned his company, Fleet Pride, as the platform for an industry roll up by aggressively modernizing his business systems and processes. He took most of the value offered by the financial buyers in cash and left a little in the new firm's stock. He stayed with the company for two years during the transition. But his lifestyle was secure and he had a stake for another new venture.

In a strategic alliance, founders can attract badly needed capital, in substantial amounts, from a large company interested in their technologies. Typically, a strategic alliance involves some exchange of value. For example, Exabyte, a storage device company out of Colorado, agreed to a strategic alliance with Sony. In exchange for Asian distribution rights, Sony opened up its manufacturing facilities to make the Exabyte product, greatly saving on capital needed for rapid expansion. Such arrangements often can also lead to complete buyouts of the founders downstream.

Outright Sale

Most advisors view outright sale as the ideal route to go, because upfront cash is preferred over most stock (even though the latter can result in a tax-free exchange).[6] In a stock-for-stock exchange, the problem is the volatility and unpredictability of the stock price of the purchasing company. Many entrepreneurs have been left with a fraction of the original purchase price when the stock price of the buyer's company declined steadily. Often the acquiring company wants to lock key management into employment contracts for up to several years. Whether this makes sense depends on the goals and circumstances of the individual entrepreneur.

Public Offering

Probably the most sacred business school cow of them all—other than the capital cow—is the notion of taking a company public.[7] The vision or fantasy of having one's venture listed on one of the stock exchanges, even over-the-counter trading, arouses passions of greed, glory, and greatness. For many would-be entrepreneurs, this aspiration is unquestioned and enormously appealing. Yet, for all but a chosen few, taking a company public, and then living with it, may be far more time and trouble—and expense—than it is worth.

After the stock-market crash of October 1987, the market for new issues of stock shrank to a fraction of the robust IPO market of 1986 (and even the markets of 1983 and 1985, as well). The number of new issues and the volume of IPOs did not rebound—instead they declined between 1988 and 1991. Then in 1992 and into the beginning of 1993 the IPO window opened again after a long dormant period. During this IPO frenzy, "small companies with total assets under $500,000 issued more than 68 percent of all IPOs."[8] Previously, small companies had not been as active in the IPO market. (Companies such as Lotus, Compaq, and Apple Computer do get unprecedented attention and fanfare, but these firms were truly exceptions.)[9] The SEC tried "to reduce issuing costs and registration and reporting burdens on small companies, and began by simplifying the registration process by adopting Form S-18, which applies to offerings of less than $7,500,000, and reduced disclosure requirements."[10] Similarly, Regulation D created "exemptions from registration up to $500,000 over a twelve-month period."[11]

This cyclical pattern repeated itself again during the mid-1990s into 2002. As the dot-com, telecommunications, and networking explosion accelerated from 1995 to 2000, the IPO markets exploded as well. In June 1996, for instance, nearly two hundred small companies had initial public offerings, and the pace remained very strong through 1999, even into the first two months of 2000. Once the NASDAQ began its collapse in March 2000, the IPO window virtually shut. In 2001 there were months when not a single IPO occurred, and for the year IPOs numbered well under one hundred! In the United States in 2002 and 2003 IPOs again numbered less than one hundred. As we write this book in mid-2004, it appears that the IPO market is starting to open once again. The lesson is clear: depending upon the IPO market for a harvest is a highly cyclical strategy, which can cause both great joy and disappointment. Such is the reality of the stock markets. Exhibits 9.1 and 9.2 show this pattern vividly.

There are several advantages to going public, many of which relate to the ability of the company to fund its rapid growth. Public equity markets provide access to long-term capital, while also meeting subsequent capital needs. Companies may use the proceeds of an IPO to

Exhibit 9.1 Number of Recent IPOs

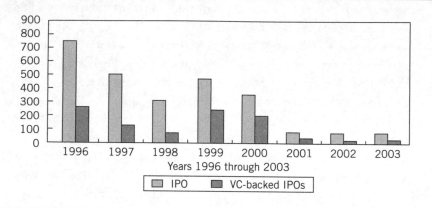

Source: Thomson Financial, May 2004.

Exhibit 9.2 Recent IPO $ Millions

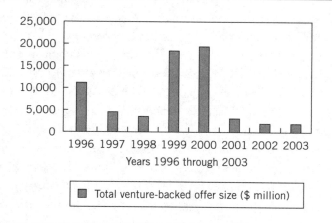

Source: Thomson Financial, May 2004.

expand the business in the existing market or to move into a related
market. The founders and initial investors might be seeking liquidity,
but it is important to note that SEC restrictions limiting the timing and
the amount of stock that the officers, directors, and insiders can dispose

of in the public market are increasingly severe. As a result, it can take several years after an IPO before a liquid gain is possible. Additionally, some entrepreneurs believe, a public offering not only increases public awareness of the company but also contributes to the marketability of the products.

However, there are also some disadvantages to being a public company. For example, 50 percent of the computer software companies surveyed by Steven Holmberg (American University) agreed that the focus on short-term profits and performance results was a negative attribute of being a public company.[12] Also, because of the disclosure requirements, public companies lose some of their operating confidentiality, not to mention having to support the ongoing costs of public disclosure, audits, and tax filings. With public shareholders, the management of the company has to be careful about the flow of information because of the risk of insider trading. When weighing the positive and negative attributes, you may find it useful to review the Boston Communications Group, Inc., website (bcgi.net) to identify the key components of the IPO process and to assess which investment bankers, accountants, lawyers, and advisors might be useful in making this decision.

Beyond the Harvest

A majority of highly successful entrepreneurs seem to accept a responsibility to renew and perpetuate the system that has treated them so well. Somehow they are keenly aware that our unique American system of opportunity and mobility depends in large part upon a self-renewal process. There are many ways in which this happens. Some of the following data often surprise people:

- **College endowments.** Entrepreneurs are generous and frequent contributors to college endowments, scholarship funds, and the like. At Babson College, for example, one study showed that as many as eight times as many entrepreneurs, compared to all other graduates, made large gifts to their colleges.[13] One cannot walk on any college or university campus in America and not help but notice the huge number of dorms, classroom buildings, arts centers, and athletic facilities named for the contributor. In virtually every case these contributors are entrepreneurs whose highly successful companies enabled them to make major gifts of stock to their alma mater, like Arthur M. Blank (Home Depot), Daniel Gerber (Gerber baby food), and Franklin W. Olin (engineer, entrepreneur, and philanthropist). At MIT over half of the endowment comprised gifts of founders' stock. Today that figure is probably even higher.

- **Community activities.** Entrepreneurs who have harvested their ventures very often reinvest their leadership skills and money in such community activities as symphony orchestras, museums, and local colleges and universities. These entrepreneurs lead fund-raising campaigns, serve on boards of directors, and devote many hours to other voluntary work—particularly in the United States. British entrepreneur Duncan Collins is astonished by the level and intensity of philanthropy in the United States: "In many parts of the world entrepreneurs might have a community interest to which they contribute. In America successful people devote large chunks of their time to serving on the boards and contributing to not-for-profit organizations."

- **Investing in new companies.** Postharvest entrepreneurs also reinvest their efforts and resources in the next generation of entrepreneurs and their opportunities. Successful entrepreneurs seem to know that perpetuating the system is far too important, and too fragile, to be left to anyone else. They have learned the hard lessons.

The innovation, the job creation, and the economic renewal and vibrancy are all results of the entrepreneurial process. Government does not cause this complicated and little-understood process, though it facilitates and/or impedes it. It is *not* caused by the stroke of a legislative pen, though it can be ended by one. Rather, entrepreneurs, investors, and hard-working people in pursuit of opportunities create it.

Fortunately, entrepreneurs seem to accept a disproportionate share of the responsibility to make sure the process is renewed. And, judging by the new wave of entrepreneurship in the United States, both the marketplace and society once again are prepared to allocate the rewards to entrepreneurs that are commensurate with their acceptance of responsibility and delivery of results.

Conclusion

Entrepreneurs thrive on the challenges and satisfactions of the game: it is a journey, not a destination. First and foremost, successful entrepreneurs strive to build a great company; wealth follows that process. It is clear that, as Ray Kroc stated, "Your company is green and growing or ripe and rotting." A growing company will have many more harvest options than a stagnant one. Indeed, the company that does not grow might very well find itself forced into a sale during a crisis.

Harvest options mean more than simply selling the company, and these options are an important part of the entrepreneur's know-how. Entrepreneurs understand that to perpetuate the system for future generations, they must give back to their communities and invest time and capital in the next e-generation.

Notes

1. "Parenting Magazine" and Harvard Business School Publishing case study 291-015, October 30, 1990.

2. Lawrence M. Fisher, "The Entrepreneur Employee," *New York Times*, Aug. 2, 1992, p. 10.

3. For TDC's business plan, see "Technical Data Corporation Business Plan," Harvard Business School Case 283-973 (revised November 1987). For more on TDC's progress and harvest strategy, see "Technical Data Corporation," Harvard Business School Case 283-072 (revised December 1987).

4. Steven R. Holmberg, "Value Creation and Capture: Entrepreneurship Harvest and IPO Strategies," in *Frontiers of Entrepreneurship Research: 1991*, ed. Neil Churchill et al. (Babson Park, MA: Babson College, 1991), pp. 191–205.

5. Mike Wright, Ken Robbie, Yves Romanet, and Steve Thompson, "Harvesting and the Longevity of Management Buy-outs and Buy-ins: A Four-Country Study," *Entrepreneurship Theory and Practice* 18, no. 2 (winter 1993): p. 90.

6. See several relevant articles on selling a company in David E. Gumpert, ed., *Growing Concerns* (New York: John Wiley & Sons, 1984), pp. 332–98.

7. The Big Four accounting firms, such as Ernst & Young, publish information on deciding to take a firm public, as does NASDAQ. See also Richard Salomon, "Second Thoughts on Going Live with Wall Street," *Harvard Business Review*, reprint no. 91309.

8. Seymore Jones, M. Bruce Cohen, and Victor V. Coppola, "Going Public," in *The Entrepreneurial Venture*, ed. William A. Sahlman and Howard H. Stevenson (Boston: Harvard Business School Publishing, 1992), p. 394.

9. For an updated discussion of these issues, see Constance Bagley and Craig Dauchy, "Going Public," in *The Entrepreneurial Venture*, 2nd ed., ed. Sahlman and Stevenson (Boston: Harvard Business School Publishing, 1999), pp. 404–40.

10. Seymore et al., "Going Public," p. 395.

11. Ibid.

12. Steven R. Holmberg, "Value Creation and Capture: Entrepreneurship Harvest and IPO Strategies," in *Frontiers of Entrepreneurship Research, 1991*, ed. Neil Churchill et al. (Babson Park, MA: Babson College, 1991), p. 203.

13. John A. Hornaday, "Patterns of Annual Giving," in *Frontiers of Entrepreneurship Research: 1984*, ed. J. Hornaday et al. (Babson Park, MA: Babson College, 1984).

INDEX